Praise for
FIGHT LESS, WIN MORE

"*Fight Less, Win More* is a massively useful book for just about anyone who has to deal with the desires, foibles, and idiosyncrasies of other human beings. The authors' framework turns conventional wisdom upside down: slow down to speed up, seek to understand before being understood, and make it about them instead of you. And the specific techniques will teach you how to listen—really listen—until the other person becomes your collaborator instead of your opponent."

Daniel H. Pink, #1 *New York Times* bestselling author of *To Sell Is Human, Drive,* and *The Power of Regret*

"*Fight Less, Win More* is a powerful reminder that presence and intention can shift even the hardest conversations."

Jay Shetty, #1 *New York Times* bestselling author and host of the *On Purpose* podcast

"Conflict is inevitable. Staying stuck in it isn't. What I love about this book is how it reframes negotiation as an opportunity for connection and progress—not friction. Jonathan and Derek show you how to unlock doors by listening better, responding smarter, and leading with empathy. Every founder, every leader, every person should read it."

Jason Feifer, editor-in-chief, *Entrepreneur Magazine*

"If you're a founder, you're always selling—ideas, vision, accountability. *Fight Less, Win More* gives you the exact framework to win those high-stakes conversations. No fluff. This isn't theory—it's a tactical guide for anyone who needs people to say yes."

Ryan Hogan, cofounder and CEO, Talent Harbor, and founder, Hunt a Killer

"Miscommunication isn't just costly—it's dangerous. In the world of intelligence and special operations, the difference between success and failure often comes down to communication under pressure. *Fight Less, Win More* arms you with that edge. Jonathan and Derek offer mission essential tools that help you build trust, de-escalate, influence, lead and operate—with precision and presence."

Col. Chris Costa, retired former special assistant to the president, career intelligence officer, and executive director of the International Spy Museum

"This book is a gift to every leader who's ever walked out of a conversation thinking, 'That didn't go how I hoped.' *Fight Less, Win More* gives you practical tools to create clarity, connection, and traction in every relationship. It's a must-read for any team committed to trust and transparency."
   Kelly Knight, integrator, EOS Worldwide

"In business, the toughest moments aren't always about the numbers—they're about people. *Fight Less, Win More* is a playbook for those high-pressure conversations where relationships and results hang in the balance. Jonathan and Derek don't just teach negotiation; they show you how to lead with empathy, create trust, and get to action faster. It's practical, real, and exactly the kind of book you want your whole team reading."
   Andrew Fried, commercial owner and CMO, Mint Mobile

"*Fight Less, Win More* provides a masterful framework for multigenerational families to break through some of the most challenging conversations with clarity, empathy, vulnerability, and purpose. It's an indispensable guide for families and their trusted advisors committed to achieving durable family harmony by leveraging the art of listening, the power of emotional intelligence, and the quiet strength of leading through understanding."
   Richard Wolkowitz, founder, Xylogenesis Family Office Advisory

"*Fight Less, Win More* is more than a book about negotiation—it's a guide to building trust and emotional connection. Jonathan and Derek demystify the path to creating enduring wins. A must-read for anyone committed to human-centered leadership."
   Sanyin Siang, CEO advisor and Duke University professor

FIGHT LESS
WIN MORE

FIGHT LESS WIN MORE

HOW MASTER NEGOTIATORS INFLUENCE HEARTS, MINDS, AND DEALS

JONATHAN B. SMITH
DEREK GAUNT

Cornerstone Press

CORNERSTONE PRESS

UK | USA | Canada | Ireland | Australia
India | New Zealand | South Africa

Cornerstone Press is part of the Penguin Random House group of companies whose addresses can be found at global.penguinrandomhouse.com

Penguin Random House UK,
One Embassy Gardens, 8 Viaduct Gardens, London SW11 7BW

penguin.co.uk

First published in the US by Amplify Publishing Group 2026
First published in the UK by Cornerstone Press 2026
001

Copyright © Chris Voss and Jonathan B. Smith, 2026

The moral right of the authors has been asserted

Penguin Random House values and supports copyright. Copyright fuels creativity, encourages diverse voices, promotes freedom of expression and supports a vibrant culture. Thank you for purchasing an authorised edition of this book and for respecting intellectual property laws by not reproducing, scanning or distributing any part of it by any means without permission. You are supporting authors and enabling Penguin Random House to continue to publish books for everyone. No part of this book may be used or reproduced in any manner for the purpose of training artificial intelligence technologies or systems. In accordance with Article 4(3) of the DSM Directive 2019/790, Penguin Random House expressly reserves this work from the text and data mining exception.

Printed and bound in Great Britain by Clays Ltd, Elcograf S.p.A.

The authorised representative in the EEA is Penguin Random House Ireland, Morrison Chambers, 32 Nassau Street, Dublin D02 YH68

A CIP catalogue record for this book is available from the British Library

ISBN: 978–1–529–99039–3 (hardback)
ISBN: 978–1–529–99040–9 (trade paperback)

Penguin Random House is committed to a sustainable future for our business, our readers and our planet. This book is made from Forest Stewardship Council® certified paper.

Derek: Dedicated to those still trying to figure it out.

*Jonathan: To my grandparents, Penny and Joe Smith—
curious minds, steady hearts,
and proud members of the Greatest Generation.*

CONTENTS

Foreword   xi

CHAPTER 1
You Have a Negotiation Problem   1

PART I: THE BLACK SWAN METHOD

CHAPTER 2
Tactical Empathy   21

CHAPTER 3
The 5 Levels of Listening   41

CHAPTER 4
The Laws of Negotiation Gravity   57

CHAPTER 5
Black Swans   75

PART II: THE CORE FOUR

CHAPTER 6
Labels   89

CHAPTER 7
Mirrors   111

CHAPTER 8
Dynamic Silence   117

CHAPTER 9
Summary   123

PART III: THE BEST OF THE REST

CHAPTER 10
Accusations Audit — 139

CHAPTER 11
Tone — 159

CHAPTER 12
Calibrated Questions — 171

CHAPTER 13
Encouragers — 183

CHAPTER 14
"I" Messages and the Phases of No — 189

PART IV: THE NEXT LEVEL

CHAPTER 15
Negotiator Personality Types — 207

CHAPTER 16
Proof of Life — 233

CHAPTER 17
Three Types of Agreement — 249

CHAPTER 18
No-Oriented Questions — 257

Conclusion — 265

APPENDIX
AI as a Tactical Empathy Tool — 271

Tactical Empathy Logbook — 273
Acknowledgments — 283
About the Authors — 287

FOREWORD

You have a negotiation problem: You haven't read this book.

You've read *Never Split the Difference* and want the next perfect read. Here it is.

It doesn't matter if you're closing a multimillion-dollar deal, managing an unruly toddler, or trying to get your team to rally around a new initiative—you are negotiating every single day. And if you don't think you are, that just means you're already losing.

For years since *Never Split the Difference* was published, people have asked me a simple yet revealing question: "Chris, what's the biggest mistake people make in negotiations?" My answer never changes: **"They don't realize they're in one."**

And that's why this book is going to change the way you see the world.

Jonathan B. Smith and Derek Gaunt are handing you something that doesn't exist anywhere else—the missing operations manual for *Never Split the Difference*. This isn't theory. This isn't guesswork. What you have in your hands is the battle-tested, proven system built from high-stakes negotiations where failure wasn't an option. It's been forged in real hostage crises, then refined everywhere from boardrooms to bedrooms, and sharpened through thousands of hours of training and coaching by The Black Swan Group.*

We built the Black Swan Method™ on a simple but powerful truth: **Emotion drives decision-making.** You don't overcome emotion with logic. You don't win by arguing harder. You win by making the other side feel understood. The minute you grasp that, you have an edge that 99 percent of negotiators will never have.

And that's where this book comes in.

Derek has spent decades teaching the ability to understand and influence people at a level they don't even realize. Derek started as a hostage negotiator with the city of Alexandria, Virginia, then became the most influential hostage negotiator in the Washington, DC, region, then became the Head of Coaching and Negotiation Training with The Black Swan Group, the company I cofounded with my son Brandon Voss.

Jonathan is The Black Swan Group's EOS† coach. When he saw what we were doing in negotiation while he was teaching us EOS, he became a relentless practitioner of The Black Swan Method. He has taken these skills and run with them. He's masterfully applied them to everything from corporate negotiations to everyday interactions.

Together, these two gentlemen are giving you not just the tools but the mindset to take control of every conversation you walk into.

But let me warn you: This book isn't about tricks. It's not about fast-talking or getting people to say yes. If that's what you're after, you're in the wrong place. This is about making better deals, strengthening relationships, and uncovering the hidden dynamics that dictate human behavior.

---

* www.blackswanltd.com.

† Entrepreneurial Operating System is a registered trademark owned by EOS Worldwide, https://www.eosworldwide.com/.

If you've ever walked away from a negotiation thinking, *I should've handled that better*, this book is for you. If you've ever felt ignored, dismissed, or outmaneuvered, this book is for you. If you want to protect yourself, your business, and your future from bad deals, this book is for you.

If you've taken my course on MasterClass[*], this book is for you.

If you love *Never Split the Difference*, **this book is for you**.

What you're about to learn will give you an unfair advantage in every interaction. And once you see how powerful it is, you'll never negotiate the same way again.

CHRIS VOSS

author of *Never Split the Difference*
and CEO of The Black Swan Group

---

[*] "Chris Voss Teaches the Art of Negotiation," MasterClass, accessed April 30, 2025, https://masterclass.com/chrisvoss.

JOIN THE BLACK SWAN COMMUNITY

Negotiation is a perishable skill. If you're not training it, you're losing it.

Just like an elite athlete sharpens their edge through constant repetitions, great negotiators must practice to stay sharp under pressure.

The principles in *Never Split the Difference* laid the foundation. *Fight Less, Win More* builds on it—deepening the strategy, sharpening the tools, and raising the bar. But books don't train behavior. Reps do. Feedback does. Live-fire practice does.

Scan the QR code below to take the next step with The Black Swan Group and turn what you've learned into instinct.—*Chris Voss*

CHAPTER 1

YOU HAVE A NEGOTIATION PROBLEM

"I regret to inform you that you are not eligible to participate in this year's program."

I (all first-person references in the book will be to Jonathan) froze midstep on the Riverside Park walking path, oblivious to the Manhattan joggers and cyclists giving me dirty looks as they swerved around me. I squinted at my phone—surely the blazing summer sun was playing tricks on my eyes. Rejected by the FBI Citizens Academy? And not just rejected but *ineligible*? How could this be?!

I had been looking forward to this thing for months—years, actually. It was an exclusive program designed to give civilian leaders an inside view of the FBI, and I had wanted to do it for ages. Just to apply, I had to be nominated by an FBI employee, and my acceptance was conditional on approval by the leader of the New York City field office. I had a sponsor inside the FBI as well as multiple other FBI connections to vouch for me, so I was sure my application would be accepted.

Apparently not. According to this email, I hadn't passed the background check … but that couldn't be right. My record was blemish-free. This had to be a mistake. Could they have mixed me up with some other John Smith? It wouldn't be the first time in my life that having the most common name in the phone book had caused confusion (thanks, Mom and Dad).

I'll be honest—I'm not a naturally patient guy. In fact, I was incensed. Offended. Horrified. For the first time in my life, I had been accused of being a criminal, and by the FBI no less. I wanted to come out swinging in defense of my good (if common) name, even though I suspected this was all probably just an innocent mistake.

You know the feeling. How often does a day go by when you don't encounter *someone* who stands in your way somehow—someone whose desires seem to conflict with yours?

Let us paint you a picture. (We're making a boatload of assumptions about your life here, but just go with it for a minute.)

Imagine it's a typical Tuesday at 6:00 a.m. Your day starts at the coffee shop, where another customer is blocking the whole coffee station as she pours her morning cup of joe. When you reach across her to get the cream, she growls and gives you the side eye … which seems to set the tone for the day.

At the morning team meeting, you float a great idea you've been pondering for weeks, but your colleagues disregard your input and unceremoniously move to the next agenda item. No one acknowledges the value of your proposal, even though you articulated it so clearly.

Later, you reach out yet again to the big client whose contract is up for renewal. They said they wanted to continue working with your company, but they haven't answered your calls or emails for weeks. You want to talk to your boss about it, but you're afraid he'll blame and criticize you instead of helping to solve the problem. You're up for a promotion soon, and losing this account might sidetrack the whole process, so you decide not to say anything.

You come home mentally exhausted, only to have yet another go-around with your kids over doing their homework and picking up their messes. You wonder how many times you can have the same argument without losing your mind completely. Groundhog Day!

Then your partner, seemingly oblivious to your stress, asks you to run a bunch of extra errands tomorrow. You reluctantly agree to it because you don't have the energy to fight, but inside, you're fuming. Can't they see that you have enough on your plate already?

OK, that terrible Tuesday we just described might be a little over the top. You probably don't have *that* many stress-inducing interactions on any given day. It might not be far off, though, especially if your daily life includes a lot of people—strangers, colleagues, customers, family, and more. The more time you spend around others, the more opportunities there are for unintended conflicts like these.

So, think back on the past week. At any point, did a conversation leave you feeling misunderstood, marginalized, or ignored? Did you struggle to get what you wanted or needed from others? Did you experience conflict or misalignment with others that sparked negative emotions? Did you avoid a conversation you knew would be unpleasant? Did your own frustration, anger, or anxiety make a conversation harder than it needed to be?

If the answer is yes, you have a negotiation problem.

EVERY CONVERSATION IS A NEGOTIATION

That diagnosis might surprise you. You probably think of negotiation as something that happens when people in suits sit down at a table to hammer out a deal or when FBI agents get on the phone with a hostage-taking bank robber. Would you be opposed to us painting you a much broader picture?

A negotiation is any interaction where someone wants or needs something.

Sometimes it's you who wants or needs something. Sometimes it's the other person. Sometimes it's both. Negotiations can happen anytime, anywhere, with anyone. When you have to decide who gets the bathroom first in the morning, it's a negotiation. When your kid doesn't want to go to bed, it's a negotiation. When you need to check in early at your hotel, it's a negotiation.

Even when you order a drink at Starbucks, it's a negotiation. At TED2012, Frank Warren—the founder of PostSecret—shared some of the secrets that had been anonymously mailed to him or posted on his website over the years. One particularly memorable one was a cut-up Starbucks cup that said, "I give decaf to customers who are RUDE to me!"[*] What seems like a simple transaction is actually a negotiation: You *want* your coffee made right, and the barista *wants* respect, kindness, and a tip.

Whether you realize it or not, your day is a series of negotiations—or as we often call them, sensitive conversations. We use that term because whenever someone wants or needs something, negative emotions are triggered. Wanting something from someone makes you feel vulnerable because they have the power to fulfill (or *not* fulfill) your desire. On the flip side, someone wanting something from *you* makes you feel threatened because giving it to them might mean losing something valuable, even if it's just your time or attention.

The moment "I want" or "I need" is in someone's head, everybody instinctively braces to protect themselves—which is why sensitive conversations can be such a huge source of stress.

What most people don't realize is that the typical approach to sensitive conversations massively amplifies that stress. By the typical approach, we mean focusing on what you want and using facts, logic, and reason

---

[*] Ben Lillie, "Secrets Can Take Many Forms: Frank Warren at TED2012," TED Blog, February 29, 2012, https://blog.ted.com/secrets-can-take-many-forms-frank-warren-at-ted2012/.

to convince the other person to give it to you. (And if that fails, sometimes falling back on less honorable tactics like passive aggression, pouting, pleading, bullying, or screaming.)

On the surface, that probably seems like a sensible way to navigate the situation. After all, how are you going to get what you want if you don't focus on it? And how are they going to understand why they should give it to you if you don't *explain* it to them?

In reality, though, this approach usually alienates the other person and makes it hard, if not impossible, to get the outcome you want. Even if you *do* get what you want, the relationship often gets damaged because your counterpart is left with a bad taste in their mouth. That breeds resentment, which makes every future negotiation with that person more difficult. If you examine the sensitive conversations in your life—especially the ones that happen repeatedly—you'll start to recognize this pattern. The harder you try to explain and convince, the harder the other person pushes back. It's a vicious cycle that leaves both sides frustrated and risks undermining the relationship.

So, what are you supposed to do instead?

A LEARNABLE SUPERPOWER

You're not going to like our answer.

It's probably going to sound completely ridiculous.

It may go against all your instincts and training.

You're going to think there's no way we're being serious.

You will want to close this book and throw it in the trash.

In short, the first step in any negotiation is to …

Make the other person feel heard and understood.

This is the essence of Tactical Empathy—the calibrated application of emotional intelligence to recognize and express the perspective of your counterpart. Think of it as the art and science of influencing others by articulating what they're thinking and feeling, *without* necessarily agreeing, disagreeing, or sympathizing.

Sympathy and empathy are very different. When you sympathize, you feel what they feel. When you empathize, you see what they see—you understand their perspective, whether you agree with it or not. Sympathy is totally unnecessary and can even hinder you in a negotiation. Empathy, on the other hand, is *essential*.

What's the difference between regular empathy and Tactical Empathy? In general, empathy is about seeing things from the other person's point of view. *Tactical* Empathy is about using that view to make the other person feel understood, thereby opening them up to communicating honestly and collaborating productively with you.

Tactical Empathy allows you to navigate sensitive conversations in a manner that focuses on the expressed and unexpressed needs of your counterpart as much as your own, in order to strengthen your relationships instead of undermining them. Not only does it vastly increase your chances of getting what you want, but it also makes the other person feel heard so that they *willingly* give it to you. It builds a healthy relationship on a foundation of mutual respect and trust, which comes with immeasurable benefits. First of all, your future negotiations, conversations, interactions, and engagements with that person will be far more pleasant and less stressful. But beyond that, a healthy relationship can give you access to support, resources, connections, and opportunities that would otherwise have been out of your reach.

In many ways, Tactical Empathy flies in the face of what we all do naturally. We're programmed to view the world through our own perspective. Of course we are—we live inside our own heads, after all. We're constantly immersed in what *we* observe, think, and feel. What's going on in other people's heads is a complete mystery in comparison. It takes a huge amount of skill, effort, and attention to genuinely understand another person's point of view, so it's no surprise we rarely take the time to do it.

At the same time, we all share the same deep-seated desire for another human being to understand us. It's not just psychological—it's biological.

When we don't feel understood in a conversation, the other person becomes a threat; they don't get us, so they're likely to act against our best interests. That triggers a stress response, with all the hormones and other physiological effects that come with it. We think less clearly. We misinterpret. We overreact. It's not pretty.

When we *do* feel understood, the opposite happens. Our brains hit us with hormones that make us feel relaxed, rewarded, and closer to the other person. We start to trust them. Our minds open up to receiving and processing new information. We feel more inclined to share information. Our judgment is no longer clouded by negative emotions.

Who would you rather negotiate with—someone who is defensive and closed off, or someone who is calm and open to your perspective?

Now you're starting to see the value of making other people feel understood. Until you do that, they're not interested in anything you have to say. But the minute you satisfy this universal need, you open the door to a whole new level of communication and collaboration.

This concept will completely change the way you interact with the world. Your instinct to judge and jump to conclusions will be replaced by *curiosity*. Instead of taking what people say and do at face value, you'll start to look for the unspoken motivations behind those behaviors—the emotions, beliefs, desires, and fears they desperately want you to understand but aren't expressing to you.

Being able to uncover and articulate those things is a learnable superpower—and when we say superpower, we mean it. When you use these skills correctly, it will feel like you can read minds, predict the future, and inject truth serum into anyone you talk to. Other people will be almost magically inclined to cooperate with you, agree with you, and follow your advice. You'll feel like a comic book superhero, only you don't have to be bitten by a radioactive spider or born with mutant genes to have these powers.

The craziest part is that you don't even have to get it right. Even if you take a wild guess at what someone is thinking and feeling, and it's dead wrong, they still open up to you because you *tried*. You expressed genuine interest in them, which instantly makes them feel good. It's like trying to speak a foreign language—even if you're not fluent, your counterpart appreciates the attempt. Most people don't get that kind of attention from anyone in their lives, not even their loved ones. They are *starving* to feel understood, and when you can do that for them, they'll engage with you in a way you never imagined ... and help you achieve outcomes you never thought possible.

THIS MIGHT SOUND FAMILIAR

If you've heard of Tactical Empathy before, it's probably because you read *Never Split the Difference: Negotiating As If Your Life Depended On It* by Chris Voss (with Tahl Raz). That book swept the business world when it came out in 2016, quickly becoming a *Wall Street Journal* bestseller by challenging long-standing principles of conventional business negotiation with proven strategies from the high-stakes world of hostage negotiation. Since then, it has sold over four million copies and formed the foundation of Chris's negotiation training company, The Black Swan Group.

Derek Gaunt (coauthor of this book) knew Chris long before all that. They met in 2000, when Chris moved to the DC area to join the elite Crisis Negotiation Unit at the FBI. At the time, Derek was a hostage negotiator with the police department in Alexandria, Virginia, and he had established an association to coordinate hostage negotiator training and operations across the many city, county, state, and federal jurisdictions in the DC area. After being introduced through a mutual friend, Chris became involved in the association and invited Derek to speak at the FBI's national negotiation training course. They quickly became friends and trained together frequently until Chris left the FBI to start The Black Swan Group in 2007.

A few years later, Derek got a call from Chris. Black Swan had been hired to train a group of executives from the China Development Bank at the Goethe University School of Business in Frankfurt, Germany. Chris had a conflict and wanted Derek to fill in for him. Fly to a foreign country (Germany) to teach a foreign language (Tactical Empathy) to people from another foreign country (China) who didn't even speak English? With virtually no preparation? Derek reluctantly agreed, fully expecting the event to be a disaster.

Instead, it was a huge success—so good that the following year, the organizer requested Derek again instead of Chris. Derek has been a Black Swan coach ever since, traveling the world to teach Tactical Empathy to individuals and organizations of all kinds. He joined the company full-time after retiring from law enforcement in 2017, and in 2022 he released his own book, *Ego, Authority, Failure: Using Emotional Intelligence like a Hostage Negotiator to Succeed as a Leader*.

I met Chris in 2013 at the Tower Club, a business club in DC. A mutual acquaintance introduced us because he thought I might be able to help Chris with a negotiation challenge. Chris was doing some work in Abu Dhabi, and the client was dragging their feet on paying the contract. I had a $100 million contract in Abu Dhabi at the time and had spent the last eight years on the ground there, so I knew the business and cultural landscape well. One of my core values is to help first, so I was happy to help Chris navigate the situation.

I didn't have the slightest clue that I was giving negotiation advice to a professor of negotiation at Georgetown University known as *the* FBI hostage negotiator (as his Instagram handle—@thefbinegotiator—clearly states). That didn't become clear until later, when Chris invited me and the team from Abu Dhabi onto the boat that was his home at the time. We took a cruise to the Georgetown Waterfront, and it was the beginning of a wonderful friendship and partnership.

As it turned out, I was a believer in Tactical Empathy before I even knew what it was. It had been a central factor in my success as an entrepreneur, helping me build a mini-multinational security firm in the Middle East, despite having no previous ties in the region. When I met Chris, I had recently exited my business and was looking to make my next move. I became completely engrossed in what Chris was teaching, and I ended up leveraging my entrepreneurial experience and Black Swan skills to become one of the top Entrepreneurial Operating System® (EOS) Implementers in the world. As an Expert EOS Implementer, I guided The Black Swan Group in developing its business model and eventually became a Black Swan coach as well.

In the years since *Never Split the Difference* came out, the demand for our negotiation training has exploded. Black Swan coaches have traveled the world and taught tens of thousands of people how to use Tactical Empathy. Major companies, including Amazon, have made the book required reading for their employees. There's even a course on the MasterClass platform that is featured on Delta's in-flight entertainment system.

The training filled a crucial gap: The stories in the book resonated strongly with people. But applying the skills in their own businesses and lives was no cakewalk. They didn't know where to begin or if they were doing it right. They didn't know how to use the skills consistently enough to make them habitual. They needed someone to break everything down in a very practical way and explain exactly what to do and what not to do.

For eight years, our in-person and online training have done that job exceptionally well … but it's expensive. We don't want cost to be a barrier to skills that can make such a transformative difference in your everyday life.

So, we created this book. It combines Derek's unparalleled understanding of the skills with my obsessive practice of them in everyday life and business. He's the professor who teaches these skills to thousands of people every year; I'm the practitioner who puts them to the test in sensitive conversations of all varieties. Together, we'll be your guides on the journey to mastering Tactical Empathy.

WHAT TO EXPECT

Keep reading and you'll find a thorough guide to the fundamentals of Tactical Empathy. It includes not only detailed explanations of the skills but also the principles of a Tactical Empathy mindset, low-stakes ways to practice the skills every day, and plenty of examples of real-life applications of these skills. Those four things are all part of the proven process for mastering the Black Swan skills. It's not a linear process but a cyclical one, with four steps:

1. **Learn:** Build the foundation by engaging with resources—like this book—about the principles and skills.
2. **Adopt:** Let go of the traditional combative approach to negotiation and adopt the Tactical Empathy frame of mind for every sensitive conversation.
3. **Practice:** Practice the skills in low-stakes environments, log your efforts, and reflect on them to discover where you excel and where you need more work.
4. **Apply:** Use your skills in real situations where the pressure is on and the stakes are real.

It's tempting to think that just by reading this book, you'll have a solid grasp on these skills. The truth is, there's no value in reading this book unless you're committed to following through with the other three steps in this process. It's the mindset shift, the practice, and the application that make a real impact on your life. You'll go through this cycle over and over with the different skills, adding to your repertoire with each pass.

We can't overstate the importance of this process. As the ancient Greek poet Archilochus said, "We don't rise to the level of our expectations; we fall to the level of our training." Tactical Empathy is most powerful—and most necessary—when the stakes are high and negative emotions are at play. Under that kind of pressure, you're not going to be cool and clearheaded enough to use some strange new technique that still makes you uncomfortable. You're going to fall back on your most automatic habits—the ones that alienate people and undermine relationships. In other words, if you don't seize every opportunity to practice Tactical Empathy *before* the big moments, you won't be able to pull it off when you really need it.

Fortunately, opportunities to practice Tactical Empathy are everywhere, and this book will show you how to spot and use them to your advantage. If you consistently do the work, soon you'll find that a huge amount of the stress around your interactions with other people simply disappears. It becomes easier to be heard, influence others, make group decisions, resolve conflicts, repair mistakes, and of course, get what you want from other people. In time, you'll be able to approach *any* conversation with confidence and calm—yes, even the ones that make you sweat, squirm, and scream today.

That said, we need to be perfectly clear about a few things.

What you're learning here is tools for your tool kit, not a road map or script. You're probably going to be frustrated that we're not giving you a clear step-by-step sequence to get what you want in any situation. The reality is, Tactical Empathy simply doesn't work that way. Everything is predicated on what the other person is saying and doing. It's like being at bat in a baseball game: Your swing depends on what the pitcher throws. That's why we can't tell you in advance exactly what to say or do in every situation. We can only teach you about the tools at your disposal—how they work, when to use which one, and most importantly, how to use them well.

You might be expecting this book to help you negotiate more lucrative business deals. It will, but what we're teaching goes way beyond money; it's about becoming a master of relationships in all spheres of life. It's true; Chris Voss originally started The Black Swan Group and wrote *Never Split the Difference* to help businesses stop leaving money on the table. But we can't even begin to count the number of clients who have told us that our training transformed their personal lives in ways they never expected. We've seen Tactical Empathy bring estranged relatives back together, save failing marriages, and end chronic battles between parents and children.

The point is, these are not just business skills. They're life skills, and the more you practice them in all contexts and with all people, the more transformative they'll be. This is especially true if engaging in sensitive conversations with others is a major pain point for you. If you find it hard to talk to people, if you struggle to get along or collaborate with others, if you feel chronically misunderstood … what you learn in this book will transform your *whole life*.

From what we've told you so far, you might be thinking that Tactical Empathy is just about being nice all the time. In fact, the beauty of Tactical Empathy is that it allows you to be extraordinarily assertive and direct *without* offending people. It lets you tell someone to knock it off without insulting their pride. It lets you deliver bad news, disagreement, or criticism and have it actually be heard and accepted. If you're a forceful person whose words often spark resistance, anger, or pain in others, Tactical Empathy will help you deliver those messages more effectively. If you're a more sensitive person who avoids being direct for fear of hurting others, it will help you say what needs to be said.

You might also be worried that Tactical Empathy sounds a lot like manipulation. As we always say, the difference between influence and manipulation is intent. Yes, the ultimate purpose of Tactical Empathy is to influence others, but for the skills to work, the empathy has to be genuine. If you think you can fake curiosity and interest in other people to get them to do what you want, think again. People can smell a fake a mile away. In fact, using Tactical Empathy in a disingenuous way will do more damage to your relationships than not using it at all. It's a beautiful irony that in order to have more influence over people, you actually have to become a more thoughtful, considerate, and engaged person.

One final warning: Tactical Empathy will slow you down ... but it's slowing you down to speed you up. It takes time to uncover the true motivations of other people, and it's going to feel like you're taking the long way to your destination. However, it's actually a shortcut. Tactical Empathy is not about getting what you want *now*; it's about building the relationship so the other person feels good once they've given it to you. By spending the first 70 to 80 percent of the conversation on the other person, you save time on the back end, when empathy is reciprocated and collaboration becomes possible. You save even more time in future conversations, when your good relationship makes the other person far more likely to be in a collaborative state of mind instead of a combative one. Tactical Empathy is a long game; if you're looking for instant gratification, you'll be disappointed.

A famous meditation teacher, Maharishi Mahesh Yogi, once said that if just 1 percent of the population practiced transcendental meditation, the whole world would be a more peaceful place.* We think something similar can be said of Tactical Empathy. It's not just a set of communication skills. It's a way of life that takes you out of your own head and focuses your attention on what other people are thinking and feeling.

---

* Bob Roth, "Maharishi on 'The 1% Effect'—How Just a Small Percentage of People Can Change the World: Transcendental Meditation® Blog," Transcendental Meditation Blog, May 12, 2012, https://usa.tm.org/blog/maharishi/maharishi-on-the-1-effect/.

That simple act, even when you only do it for a few minutes a day, changes you. You become more tolerant and understanding. You're less quick to offend and anger. Your relationships become deeper and more joyful.

It's not a stretch to imagine that if just 1 percent of us could do that, the world would be a better place. Ultimately, we each live an interdependent existence: We rely on other people, and other people rely on us. None of us can accomplish much of anything alone. So, the quality of your relationships and communication can make or break your daily life at work, at home, and everywhere in between.

Which brings me back to that horrifying email from the FBI. I was fuming on the inside ... but because of my Black Swan training, I knew better than to act on those feelings. Valid as my indignation might have seemed to me at that moment, it would only hold me back from getting what I wanted.

Instead, I put on my Black Swan hat—not the actual baseball cap with the company name on it, but the figurative one that puts me in a Tactical Empathy frame of mind. I wrote a very polite, deferential response expressing my surprise at the background check results, given that I had no criminal record and had recently passed a background check to get a traveler redress number from the Department of Homeland Security. I pointed out that my common name sometimes led to mix-ups, then asked the key question: "How hard would it be for you to clarify the reason for my ineligibility?"[*]

Less than twenty-four hours later, I had my answer: They had entered my date of birth incorrectly when running the background check. The other John Smith was a convicted felon (of course). After running it again with the correct date, they saw that my record was pristine. I was in fact

---

[*] This is a No-Oriented Question, as you'll learn in chapter 18.

fully eligible for the program, and I would be receiving an official acceptance email by close of business that day.

A few years earlier, that story might have had a very different ending. As I said, patience isn't one of my natural virtues, and on top of that, my pride was wounded. Back then I probably would have sent a scathing email accusing them of making a mistake and insisting that they run the background check again. Would I have gotten what I wanted? Doubtful. Certainly not in less than a day. And even if I had, the program coordinator would have pegged me as an obnoxious, entitled jerk, and who knows how that might have come back to bite me later.

What I did might seem like a simple thing. After all, what's so hard about writing a polite email? But as you'll soon learn, the skills that went into that email—including the presence of mind not to follow my instincts—go way beyond politeness. They represent a completely different way of approaching human interaction, one that makes it possible to get what you want *and* make other people feel good.

By picking up this book, you've taken the first step to adopting that approach. Now, don't expect to read it cover to cover in a few hours and suddenly be a master of Tactical Empathy. As with any skill, it takes time and consistent practice to get this in your bones so it feels natural and effortless. This book is your companion on that journey. Don't let it become a decoration on your shelf; by the time you get to the end, we hope it's well worn, dog-eared, and full of notes that chronicle your progress in real life. Turn the page, and let's get started.

PART I

THE BLACK SWAN METHOD

Before we get to the nitty-gritty of negotiation tools and techniques, let's look at the foundational principles that underpin them. The next four chapters are all about how you approach a conversation before a single word comes out of your mouth. You're about to learn:

- Exactly what Tactical Empathy is and why it's so effective
- How to listen at a deeper level than you've ever imagined
- Ten truths about human nature you should never ignore
- How to recognize game-changing information in every conversation

CHAPTER 2

TACTICAL EMPATHY

A while back, I had to get some blood tests done. I had lab orders from two different doctors, and knowing this might cause some complications, I had confirmed multiple times with each doctor's office that the lab had my paperwork. All I had to do was go to my blood work appointment, and the orders for all my tests would be there in the computer system.

So, I showed up for my 10:15 a.m. appointment at 10:12, greeted the lab technician in my friendliest voice, and mentioned that there should be orders from two doctors.

She scrunched her nose and said, "I only see one."

Immediately, I felt my blood pressure rising. I had gotten specific assurances that the orders would be there. What the hell?

I was triggered ... but as Derek always says, we can't choose whether we get triggered. We can only choose how we respond—with an emotional outburst or with thoughtfully chosen words and actions. I could unleash my fury on the person in front of me, but she hadn't caused this problem and she might well be able to help me solve it.

I looked at her name tag: Chamel.

"Chamel ... that's an interesting name. How did you get it?"

She looked up from the computer with a smile. "I'm named after my father. I'm the firstborn of my siblings." Then, without me asking, she gave me the right phone number to call about finding my orders.

After I worked through the byzantine hospital phone system, a pleasant voice said in her Southern drawl, "This is Gabby. How can I help you?" I calmly explained the situation, and Gabby worked for fifteen minutes to resolve it, bumping me from number 18 in the queue to the top of the list. The orders were faxed through a few minutes later, and Chamel drew my blood.

Just as I was about to get out of the chair, she said, "Hold on a minute—I heard another fax come through."

Wouldn't you know it—it was the second half of the orders. So, Chamel pricked me again and filled a few more vials. We laughed about it, and I joked that she was lucky I wasn't a heroin user. She proceeded to share all sorts of stories about unusual veins and the interesting people who come through her chair. She told me I was her "most difficult" patient for the day with a smile. If I had been like a lot of New Yorkers, she admitted, she would have been reluctant to help. However, she went out of her way to ensure that I got everything I needed, even cutting her lunch break short to give me a second needle prick.

As I walked out, I handed her a twenty and told her lunch was on me.

You're probably wondering why I'm telling you this story. It doesn't sound like a negotiation. It doesn't seem like I used any Jedi mind tricks to make the situation go my way.

But that's exactly why I'm telling it—because Tactical Empathy isn't just a bag of tricks to break out when you're sitting at the negotiation table. It's a mindset. It's a way of being. It's an approach to thinking about and communicating with others that can be summed up in a few simple words ...

It's not about you.

I could have made that whole situation at the lab about me—my needs and my feelings. Instinctively, I wanted to. My righteous anger at the incompetence of others, my vast annoyance at the inconvenience of the delay—it was all there in my head. I could *taste* how good the scathing words would feel coming out of my mouth.

But none of that was going to help me get my labs done. If I had made it about me, I would have ticked off Chamel, probably gotten a not-so-gentle prick or three, and ended up having had to come back for a second appointment later, for yet another stick from a Chamel who thought I was Manhattan's biggest jerk. Bad day for me, bad day for her.

Instead, I chose not to make it about me, and not only did I get what I wanted, but I also made all the people I interacted with feel good about me. If I ever go back to that lab again (and I probably will), you can bet my friend Chamel will take good care of me.

In this book, you will learn lots of communication tools—and yes, a few Jedi mind tricks. But tools are just tools, and they can be used effectively or ineffectively, for good or for evil. Until you embrace the *mindset* of Tactical Empathy, none of the tools will work the way you want. And that mindset is rooted not in tactics but in empathy.

CROSS THE STREET

Tactical Empathy, as we said in chapter 1, is the art and science of influencing other people by making them feel understood. Let's zoom in on a key word here: *influencing*. You might think that's pretty much the same as convincing or persuading someone, but there's a world of difference.

Imagine you're standing on one side of the street and your counterpart is on the opposite side. You want them to come over to your side, so you wave, jump up and down, and yell at the top of your lungs, "Come over here! It's better, and here are eighteen reasons why! I swear, you won't regret it!" They ignore you; you scream louder. They scream back; you scream even louder.

That's what convincing looks like, and it's what most people do when they don't see eye to eye with someone else.

Influencing is the opposite: It's *crossing the street*. Instead of asking the other person to change their perspective, you volunteer to see things from their point of view first. You walk over, stand shoulder to shoulder, and say, "Oh, so this is what you're seeing from here, and that's why you think and feel this way."

"That's right," they'll say. And that's when the magic happens.

"That's right" (or "Heck yeah" or "Exactly" or "You bet" or any other phrase of emphatic agreement) is a sign of what we call *emotional buy-in*. It means they feel understood. And when they know you understand them, you're no longer a threat. They don't have to resist you anymore. That's when you can invite them to your side of the street … and they'll go willingly.

Why is this so? Why, when you tell someone a thousand good reasons to see things your way, do they do nothing but fight you, but as soon as you make them feel understood, they're all ears?

Because humans are *not* logical, to put it bluntly. As much as we might pretend or wish to operate rationally, we do not. We make decisions based primarily on emotions, then we justify them in retrospect using facts, logic, and reason.

If you're not convinced of that, just consider one famous experiment called the Ultimatum Game.[*] Imagine I take 10 crisp $1 bills from my pocket and give them to you. I say, "You just found this money, but to keep any of it, you have to split it with Derek. If he rejects your split, neither of you get to keep anything."

The only *logical* split for you to offer in this situation is $9 for you and $1 for Derek. After all, logically, you want to keep as much as

---

[*] Daniel C. Krawczyk, "Social Cognition: Reasoning with Others," in *Reasoning* (Academic Press, 2018), 283–311.

possible for yourself, and Derek should be happy to get anything at all, given that the only alternative is nothing. If you offer anything more than $1, it's an emotional decision. If Derek rejects any offer you make, it's an emotional decision.

And guess what? In study after study, people consistently offer far more than $1—often as much as $5. What's more, the recipients consistently reject offers of less than $3. You already know why—because they *feel* offended, even though they know $1 or $2 is better than $0. Revenge is a powerful motivator; people will blow up a deal when they believe they've been treated unfairly, even if doing so is not in their best interests.

We sometimes play the Ultimatum Game at our live training events with serious businesspeople who swear they operate solely based on logic. Just like everyone else, they end up making emotional decisions over $10 that's not even theirs. Just imagine the power of emotion in a $10 *million* business deal or some other high-stakes negotiation.

The people who struggle the most in negotiations are the ones who try to ignore the emotions at play or operate in spite of them. With Tactical Empathy, instead of looking at emotion as something to suppress or resist, we use it to our advantage; instead of fighting the waves, we surf them. Once you understand emotional dynamics, people become very predictable.

That's what crossing the street is all about. Most people assume that when they fail to win someone over, it's because they weren't persuasive enough … they didn't explain it right … they couldn't make the other person understand. But that's not the problem at all. When someone argues with you or ignores you, it's *not* because you're not making sense to them. It's because you didn't do a good job of removing yourself as a threat. Saying no is the ultimate defensive move. So the question isn't why you failed to convince them; it's why they feel the need to defend themselves. Why are they viewing you as a threat, and what can you do to neutralize that perceived threat?

You can cross the street and show that you get where they're coming from.

GET CURIOUS

Notice that I said *show*, not *say*. If making someone feel understood were as easy as saying, "I understand," we wouldn't need to write this book. Unfortunately, that phrase (and all its siblings, such as "I get it" and "I see what you mean") is more likely to raise the other person's guard even more. *You think you understand me? Why should I believe you? How dare you presume to know what I'm going through?*

Heaven forbid you follow "I understand" with the dreaded "but ..."

"*I understand, but you're not seeing the bigger picture ...*"

"*I see what you mean, but have you considered ...*"

"*I get that, but what about ...*"

Saying "but" is like hitting backspace, backspace, backspace: No matter what you say next, everything that came before that "but" is gone. Erased. They know you don't really understand—you just said that to shut them up so you could talk. So, to make a person feel understood, you're going to have to do more than say a few canned platitudes. You're going to have to *get curious*.

Whenever you're talking to someone, there's a *lot* to be curious about. People don't just walk into a conversation and spill everything that's on their minds. Intentionally or unintentionally, we all hide information. We pick and choose what to reveal depending on the context.

As a result, every conversation has two dynamics: the presenting dynamic and the latent dynamic. The presenting dynamic is what the other person is actually saying—the words coming out of their mouth. This is the obvious stuff, but it's just the tip of the iceberg, especially in emotional or high-stakes situations. There's a whole mountain lurking beneath the surface.

That mountain is the latent dynamic: everything they're *not* saying. What is their situation? What do they want? What are they afraid of? What are they thinking? What are they feeling? Who are they, really?

We all have incredibly powerful intuition that clues us in to these things. We can read people's body language and tone of voice. We can piece together bits of information about them into a bigger picture. If we pay attention, we can make pretty good educated guesses about what's going on below the surface.

Recognizing these things is the easy part; the hard part is articulating them. We're afraid that if we say them out loud, we'll get it wrong and offend the other person. They'll say no. They'll back out of the deal. They'll withdraw their love. They'll do whatever it is that we dread most in that moment.

That's why *showing* it is what makes all the difference. When they sense that you are mirroring their perspective—not just what they literally said but the thoughts and feelings behind what they said—*that's* when they feel understood. Their guard starts to come down; their brain stops releasing stress hormones and starts releasing bonding hormones; and they start to think, *Hey, I really like talking to you.*

The path to achieving this starts with your state of mind. Are you going to focus on your own thoughts, feelings, desires, and fears? Or are you going to get curious about what's going on in *their* head? If you choose the former, you'll stay stuck on your own side of the street. To cross the street, you have to leave your mental baggage behind and choose curiosity.

SLOW DOWN TO SPEED UP

During the COVID pandemic, the power went out at my house for five days. To prevent that nightmare from happening again, I ordered a generator. When I placed the order in July, the wait was six months; my generator was supposed to come on February 1.

February 1 rolls around, and no generator. I call the generator guy, Tom, and he says it'll be there on the 7th.

February 7, no generator. I call again, and Tom says the 14th.

February 14, still no generator. I call again, and Tom snaps that if I don't stop calling, he's not going to deliver my generator.

I want to snap back, of course. *I've waited six months for this thing already! Why can't you just tell me when it's going to come!* But if I ticked him off any more, he would disappear and I'd have to wait another eight months for a new generator from someone else.

So instead of yelling, I listened to Tom and made him feel understood. He vented for thirty minutes about his woes—how his clients were so demanding, he didn't have anyone to manage the office, the manufacturer was no help, and on and on. "Gosh, you must be awfully busy," I said. "Sounds like you're frustrated … sounds like people are being unreasonable … seems like these supply chain issues are a real pain in the neck for you." By the end of the call, he was offering me an upgraded warranty and service plan for free and promising to put my order at the top of the priority list. And guess what? My generator came in two weeks.

At that moment, my extended phone call with the generator guy felt slow. Half an hour to listen to a stranger complain? Who has time for that?

This is one of the biggest objections to using Tactical Empathy: It's "too slow." It takes time to listen to someone and make them feel understood. It seems much faster to communicate the conventional way—listening for the gist and jumping in with your needs and opinions as soon as the other person pauses for breath. If I had done that in this conversation, I would have waited another eight months for my generator. But by investing thirty minutes of my time and attention, I cut my wait time by *over 90 percent*.

That's what we mean when we say that Tactical Empathy slows you down to speed you up. By investing time up front in making your counterpart feel understood, you save time (and money and stress) in the end. I think of it as trading short-term greed for long-term greed: To get what you really want in the long term, you have to be willing to set your needs aside in the short term. If you insist on being short-term greedy, you may get to your point faster, but it will take much longer to get the end result you're aiming for. That's because you're still a threat to the other person, so they will continue to resist you at every turn—especially when resisting you takes no effort on their part.

Chamel the lab tech? Tom the generator guy? They were under no obligation to give me what I wanted. If they had just ignored my desires and gone about their work as usual, there would have been no negative consequences for them. I was the only one who stood to lose. The same goes for pretty much every gatekeeper, receptionist, concierge, or other customer service person you'll ever encounter. They might have the power to grant your wishes, but it's a lot easier to deny them. That's why we always say, "Never piss someone off who can hurt you by doing nothing."

It's also tempting to speed past Tactical Empathy when you feel you have the power in a situation. Let's say you want to acquire a company and everyone knows the company will fold unless the deal goes through. You have considerable leverage in that conversation. Why take the extra time to practice Tactical Empathy when you can get what you want without it?

Because even when this negotiation is over, the relationship isn't. You have to continue working with these people, and you made them feel like dirt. Don't think they're going to forget that. Again, revenge is a powerful motivator. As Freud put it, "Unexpressed emotions will never die. They are buried alive and will come forth later in uglier ways."* The wronged party will take every opportunity to make you feel what they felt, even if it's in small ways—stonewalling a new project, failing to pass on useful information, or taking their sweet time to respond to your messages.

On the flip side, if you choose to use Tactical Empathy anyway, you cultivate goodwill that facilitates all your future interactions with those people. When they know you have the power but you have chosen not to use it, you're showing respect and building trust. So in the future, instead of resisting you, they will happily collaborate with you and go to bat for

---

* This quote can't be traced back to an exact passage in Freud's writings, but experts generally acknowledge that it's an accurate expression of his beliefs on the subject.

you. The same goes for any situation where you hold the power, whether you're the boss, the parent, or the person holding the purse strings.

Perhaps the biggest temptation to rush past opportunities for Tactical Empathy comes from technology. We all do a huge amount of communicating via email and text messages. It's convenient, but unfortunately, it's not very conducive to Tactical Empathy. Without tone of voice, facial expressions, and body language, you just don't have enough information to understand the latent dynamic in the conversation. Your ability to recognize and articulate your counterpart's worldview—and thereby make them feel understood—is stunted.

To fully practice Tactical Empathy, you need to talk face-to-face. Go verbal. Phone calls are OK; video calls are better; in person is best. No matter how convenient it seems, the last thing you want to do is have a sensitive conversation via email or text. If the conversation starts out that way, transition it to a better medium as soon as possible.

Yes, it will feel like it takes more time up front. But remember, by using Tactical Empathy to build trust and respect, you will get that time back in the future, multiplied many times over.

MINDFULNESS, PRACTICE, AND REFLECTION

We spend most of our lives focused on what's going on inside our own heads. Tactical Empathy demands that you get out of your head and into your counterpart's head. It's not about you; it's about them. This is a massive shift. You're not just learning a skill—you're undoing decades of conditioning and replacing it with a new way of being. To succeed, you're going to need three things: mindfulness, practice, and reflection.

Mindfulness

By mindfulness, we mean the ability to be aware of what's going on in your head and to make a conscious, deliberate choice about how to respond to it. Most of the time, we just react to our thoughts and feelings without examining them. You say something that offends me; I feel angry and immediately give you a scathing retort. It feels automatic, like an impulse I can't control.

Being mindful means creating space between your emotions and your response. You say something that offends me; I feel angry; I notice my anger, recognize that this is an opportunity to practice Tactical Empathy, and choose to respond with curiosity instead of rage. That tiny pause is the key. It makes you resilient to even the harshest criticism.[*] Without it, you're a slave to your emotions. Anytime you get upset, everything you know about Tactical Empathy will go out the window, and you'll default to your old conditioning.

In The Black Swan Group, we've developed a specific practice to help you rein in your reactive emotions and approach high-pressure conversations mindfully. It's called CAVIAAR, which stands for the following steps:

- **Curiosity:** As you just learned, curiosity is the heart of Tactical Empathy. It's impossible to be genuinely curious and angry at the same time. Moving your frame of mind *toward* curiosity will automatically calm your emotions.
- **Acceptance:** In any negotiation, there's a good chance you're going to be attacked. It usually has more to do with what the other person is facing than anything you've said or done. Accept that it will happen, and when it does, don't fight it. Just let it happen—it will be over in a minute.
- **Venting:** Before you enter a sensitive conversation, take the time to clear your own head by speaking all your negative thoughts and feelings out loud. Do it with a trusted colleague, a friend, the mirror, a notebook, your dog—it

---

[*] Joseph Grenny, "How to Be Resilient in the Face of Harsh Criticism," *Harvard Business Review*, July 11, 2019, https://hbr.org/2019/06/how-to-be-resilient-in-the-face-of-harsh-criticism.

doesn't matter who, as long as they can listen without judgment.
- **Identifying:** Once you've cleared your mind, you can turn your attention to your counterpart. Do your best to identify their Negotiator Personality Type (more on this in chapter 15) and how they are approaching the conversation. The better you understand their perspective and aims, the easier it will be to stay cool.
- **Accusations Audit:** Ask yourself what negative thoughts and emotions your counterpart might have about this situation, especially about *you* (more on this in chapter 10). It's counterintuitive, but starting the conversation by saying these things out loud is the perfect way to defuse their negative emotions before they explode on you.
- **Remembering:** In the end, the other person is not your enemy. Even when their goals are totally at odds with yours, the ultimate goal is to collaborate and come to an agreement. Whenever you feel your emotions rising, remind yourself that you and your counterpart are in this together.

CAVIAAR is the go-to process for entering a state of mindfulness before a sensitive conversation, especially when you're already feeling triggered. The more often you practice it, the easier it will be to regain a sense of calm whenever your emotions threaten to pull you off track.

Practice

In addition to helping you stay calm, mindfulness also helps you notice opportunities to practice Tactical Empathy. This is crucial, because you will *not* master these skills just by reading, watching videos, or memorizing scripts. Even attending our live training programs won't do the trick. The only way to truly learn these skills is to *use* them in real life, over and over and over.

Research shows that it takes around sixty-six days to develop a new habit.* Not to become an expert, mind you, but just to build a strong enough neural pathway that the new behavior takes over the old one. And your work doesn't stop there. If you don't continue repeating the new behavior consistently, that new neural pathway will wither and disappear. In other words, Tactical Empathy is a perishable skill—if you don't use it, you lose it.

Fortunately, opportunities to practice are literally *everywhere*, in all human-to-human contact from the moment you wake up to the moment you fall asleep. Your family, your colleagues, your friends, your neighbors—everyone you interact with can be a practice partner, even if unwittingly. Even the people you might not normally strike up a conversation with, like a waiter, a cashier, or the person next to you on the subway. Each interaction in life presents an opportunity to hone your skills.

You don't have to wait for a *sensitive* conversation, either. In fact, low-stakes conversations are the best ones for practicing Tactical Empathy. The pressure is off; it's OK to try things and mess them up. That's how you learn, and the more you repeat the process, the more ingrained the skills will become. Then, when a high-stakes situation comes up, you'll have plenty of reps under your belt and you might actually be able to pull off Tactical Empathy under pressure.

Doing this practice, even when the stakes are low, will feel uncomfortable at first. It's like learning a foreign language—in the beginning, even the simplest phrases will get your tongue tied. You'll worry about sounding foolish; you'll think everyone is silently judging you; you'll be tempted to avoid opening your mouth at all.

The only way to get past this feeling is to *just keep doing it*. Keep using that new neural pathway. The more you do, the stronger it gets and the more comfortable you feel. If you've ever achieved proficiency in a second language, think back to what that process was like. It didn't happen instantly. It took

---

* Jocelyn Solis-Moreira, "How Long Does It Really Take to Form a Habit?" *Scientific American*, February 20, 2024, https://www.scientificamerican.com/article/how-long-does-it-really-take-to-form-a-habit/.

many hours of practice—not just reading textbooks but also having live, spontaneous conversations in the real world with real people.

And if you want to learn a language fast, full immersion is the best way to do it. Many years ago, when Derek was working in law enforcement, he had to learn Spanish so he could go out into the community and gather intelligence on gang activity. The department sent him to Spanish class three nights a week for three hours a night. From the moment he walked in those doors, he could only speak Spanish—that was the rule. Within four weeks, he was functionally conversational.

Tactical Empathy is no different. If you want to make progress, you have to put in the hours of practice. If you want to learn fast, you have to immerse yourself in it. And if you want to be able to use it in the real world, you have to go beyond the book.

That last part is especially important. You can study example conversations to help you understand the skills, but you can't expect to use those exact words in that exact sequence in real life. Tactical Empathy is improv, not a scripted play. You may go into a conversation with a certain plan and objective, but as they say, no battle plan ever survives first contact with the enemy.[*] Ultimately, what you need to say depends entirely on what your counterpart says to you. A script will only keep you stuck. Instead, you've got to do what improv actors do: Think, *Yes, and ...* to build on what your counterpart is giving you.

So if you picked up this book hoping for a step-by-step communication formula you could whip out to "win" any conversation, now is the time to adjust your expectations. No such thing exists. In fact, even thinking in terms of memorizing a script puts you at a disadvantage. When you're focused on remembering what you're "supposed" to say, you're taking part of your brain offline from the conversation. You're not fully listening, which is a big problem because deep listening is always the first step in making someone feel understood. (More on that in chapter 3.)

---

[*] As quoted in David Detzer, *Donnybrook: The Battle of Bull Run, 1861* (Mariner Books, 2005), 233.

Reflection

So far, we've talked about the importance of mindfulness and practice. But what about reflection? This is a key step that many people ignore, which is too bad for them because it can dramatically accelerate your learning process.

Reflection is simply taking the time to look back on your recent conversations and analyze what happened. How well did you listen? What Tactical Empathy tools did you use? How did the other person respond? Were you able to make them feel understood? If you could redo that conversation, what would you do differently?

I discovered the power of reflection when I was a brand-new Black Swan coach. I had started around the same time as a couple of other coaches, and we had weekly calls to share our experiences and learn from each other. They would ask me about the sensitive conversations I'd had in the past week, and at first, I couldn't remember. So I started keeping a Tactical Empathy Logbook. At the end of every day, I would think back and jot down notes about my use of the Black Swan skills that day.

That logbook became the single most powerful driver of progress for me. Reflecting on my practice allowed me to see patterns and crystallize the lessons I learned, both from my successes and from my mistakes. On top of that, it raised my level of awareness during conversations. The practice of analyzing sensitive conversations in retrospect actually improved my ability to analyze them in real time and make better choices about how to respond to the person in front of me.

So here's our advice to you: Start your Tactical Empathy logbook *now*. Today. We've provided a section at the end of the book for this purpose. If you're reading the digital version or you'd rather not write in your book, go get a paper notebook or start a fresh digital one and dedicate it to only this. Set aside fifteen minutes every day—maybe at the end of your workday or right before bed—to reflect on that day's conversations and write down your successes, your failures, and lessons learned.

And if you *really* want to bring that learning home, talk about it. Create a community of practice—a small group, like the one I had with my fellow Black Swan coaches, that is committed to discussing their practice of Tactical Empathy.* Meet regularly, ideally once a week, to share your experiences. This will not only hold you accountable for reflecting but also allow you to learn from other people's triumphs and mistakes, which will accelerate your progress even further.

NOT A MAGIC WAND

You might be thinking that masters of Tactical Empathy are superhuman communicators for whom every conversation is a summer breeze. In reality, Tactical Empathy is not a magic wand, and even the greatest practitioners of it are only human. So before we go any further, let's be clear about a few things.

You *will* get triggered.

As we mentioned earlier, in any sensitive conversation, chances are high that you will get attacked in some way. Your counterpart is starting out in defense mode. Until you've successfully made them feel understood, which takes time, they're liable to lash out. That attack *will* trigger negative emotions for you—anger, frustration, anxiety, self-doubt, even heartbreak. Being trained in Tactical Empathy doesn't make you immune to that.

You can't prevent being triggered, but you *can* control your response. You can choose to pause, set aside your feelings, and get curious. Instead of defending yourself, you can ask what's motivating your counterpart to attack. *What am I missing? What pressures is he under? Is he trying to manipulate me?*

This is easier to do if you're prepared. When you know the chance of attack is high and you mentally gear yourself up to expect a sting, it's easier to take it when that sting comes. That's exactly what CAVIAAR is for.

---

* "What Is a Community of Practice?" Community of Practice, accessed February 5, 2025, https://www.communityofpractice.ca/background/what-is-a-community-of-practice/.

You *won't* always get your way.

Tactical Empathy is absolutely a more effective way to influence people than the conventional approach of persuading with facts, logic, and reason. However, it is *not* a surefire way to get whatever you want from anyone in any situation. Beginners often get discouraged because they try a couple of the tools a few times and find that they "don't work," so they give up and forget about the whole thing.

Imagine trying to cut down a tree with an ax. How many swings does it take? It depends on the size of the tree, the hardness of the wood, the sharpness of the ax, and the strength of your arm. Each use of a Tactical Empathy tool is a swing of the ax. Sometimes one stroke is all you need; sometimes you need a hundred.

And sometimes, the tree is actually a steel pole and the best thing you can do is stop swinging and walk away. There are situations where no amount of Tactical Empathy will win the trust of your counterpart, usually because they have no intention of negotiating in good faith in the first place. As Derek knows well, hostage negotiators have a 93 percent success rate in getting hostage takers to surrender. The other 7 percent would rather die than surrender, so there's no talking them into anything.

You will encounter those people at some point. We call them 7 Percenters: prospective clients who have no intention of ever hiring you, "dealmakers" who don't really want a deal, and others who just want to pump you for information or waste your time. The value of Tactical Empathy in those situations is that it reveals those people for what they are and gives you the tools to exit the conversation quickly and gracefully. As Chris loves to say, It's not a sin to lose a deal; it's a sin to take a long time to lose a deal. (More on this concept, which we call Proof of Life, in chapter 16.)

So, will Tactical Empathy always get you what you want? No. What it will always get you, when used correctly, is information about your counterpart. Sometimes, that information will reveal the path forward to get what you want. Sometimes, it will reveal that getting what you want is impossible. Either way, you're better off.

You *can't* always be on.

Even for advanced practitioners, it takes energy and effort to use Tactical Empathy. It requires a high level of awareness and intense focus on the person in front of you. The more you do it, the easier it gets, but even so, it's a mental state no one can maintain indefinitely.

Years ago, Derek had just come home from an overnight shift and was trying to catch a nap in the late afternoon. At that moment, his teenage daughter called to tell him that a hubcap had just come off her car.

"Where's the hubcap?" he asked.

"It's over there by the side of the road," she said.

"Well, go get it."

"Go get it?"

"Call me when you have it," he told her, then hung up.

If he had been fully alert, he would have caught the hesitation in her voice, but he was tired, annoyed, and more focused on his own emotions than on her. As a result, he didn't realize he was asking his baby girl to cross a dangerous four-lane highway to pick up a $12 piece of plastic he could have ordered on Amazon—*not* what he would have wanted, in hindsight.

What does this tell you? When you know you have a sensitive conversation on the horizon, plan to come to it well rested and energized. Don't plan on asking your boss for a raise at the end of a long, hard week; don't try to resolve a parenting disagreement with your spouse right before bed. By the same token, give yourself time to recover after intense conversations. For example, Derek has learned not to schedule more than two private coaching sessions in a day; if he wants to bring his fullest attention and capabilities, he can't do more than that.

THE BLACK SWAN TACTICAL EMPATHY PLEDGE

Now that you've gotten your first glimpse of what Tactical Empathy is all about, we want to share something we use in our workshops to solidify the commitment to this approach: the Tactical Empathy Pledge. It includes some concepts and terms we haven't explained yet, but you know enough to get the gist, and what you don't yet know, you'll soon learn.

I will ...

stay curious,
remove myself as a threat,
proactively address expressed and unexpressed dynamics/ emotions,
listen with purpose,
and practice Tactical Empathy as my superpower.

And I will ...

test all agreements,
Proof of Life every potential opportunity,
transform conversations into lasting relationships,
and not explain without permission.

And I will ...

hunt for black swans,
make "No" work for me,
and embrace the power of emotional buy-in ("That's Right").

The purpose of this pledge is simple: to keep the spirit of Tactical Empathy at the forefront of your mind. By saying it—especially before you enter into a sensitive conversation—you remind yourself that the situation isn't about winning. It's about building trust and making the other person feel understood so they will reveal their truth and open up to your influence.

IN SHORT ...

- The Tactical Empathy mindset is simple: *It's not about you—it's about them.*
- The first step in influencing your counterpart is to *cross the street* and see the world from their perspective.
- To cross the street, you have to set aside your own thoughts and feelings and *get curious* about what's going on in your counterpart's head.
- Doing this will take more time up front, but it will *save you time* in the long run by removing their resistance to collaborating with you.
- Mastering Tactical Empathy takes three things: *mindfulness* to respond thoughtfully instead of instinctively; consistent *practice*, especially in low-stakes situations; and *reflection* to solidify the lessons learned from practice.
- Tactical Empathy is *not a magic wand*. Even when you've mastered it, you will still get triggered sometimes, you won't always get what you want, and using the skills will still require focused effort.

Mastering Tactical Empathy isn't a one-time read—it's a lifelong journey. Inside the Black Swan Community, you will find people just like you, focused on getting better every day. Scan the QR Code to join.

CHAPTER 3

THE 5 LEVELS OF LISTENING

Every year, The Black Swan Group goes on a business planning retreat. We like to have fun while we're at it, so we look for unique venues and unique activities to do while we're there—and we often leverage our networks to find those special opportunities. Last year, I called on a longtime friend of mine who had married into a powerful family in the wine industry. I was hoping he could help hook us up with the best lodging, food, and tours in California Wine Country.

He got me a meeting with the head of the family office, Brian. I assumed my friend had filled Brian in on what the call was about, and I hopped on the phone expecting a friendly chat about what The Black Swan Group should do on our retreat. To my surprise, the tone on the other end was frosty. He clearly did not want to be on this call and was trying to end it as quickly as possible.

He seemed confused about who we were, so I gave him some background about what The Black Swan Group did. That only seemed to make things worse. He cut me off, saying, "You know, I don't have any control over procurement."

There was the first clue to what was wrong. We had told him we just wanted a little help planning our retreat, and we hadn't tried to sell him anything. So why was he talking about procurement?

To follow this train of thought, I had to listen for what he *wasn't* saying. As the head of the family office, he was a crucial gatekeeper, responsible for protecting the time and resources of these busy, important people. He was probably bombarded every day by solicitations and pitches, sometimes veiled by innocent requests like ours. Could it be possible that he thought I wanted to pitch him Black Swan services? Was that why he kept trying to shut down the conversation?

I took a leap and tested my theory out loud: "You probably think we're trying to sell you consulting. We're not—we just want to come out to Wine Country and have a good time."

Instantly, his whole demeanor changed. He relaxed, smiled, and said, "Oh, we have a private party planner who does all the family events. She can help you—I'll put you in touch." He immediately introduced the party planner to our logistics coordinator, and our retreat ended up being a once-in-a-lifetime experience. The family rolled out the red carpet for us, allowing us to use their gorgeous conference center, sending us on incredible vineyard tours, and even throwing a welcome party for us at their private mansion.

This is the power of truly great listening.

In the last chapter, we introduced the concept of presenting and latent dynamics. The universal tendency is to focus on the presenting dynamic—the words coming out of the other person's mouth. That doesn't require any work, imagination, or risk-taking. The presenting dynamic is there in plain sight. There's far less awareness of the latent dynamic—what the other person is *not* saying but is almost certainly showing in some way through their tone and body language. Human intuition picks up those signals very well, but most people make the mistake of ignoring them.

To succeed with Tactical Empathy, we need to listen for the latent dynamic. Your counterpart is begging you to verbalize what they are unable or refuse to say—that's what will really make them feel understood. That's why we're dedicating this entire chapter to the skill of listening.

There are five levels of listening. Most people operate on the first few levels virtually all the time; even people who think they're "good" listeners rarely go beyond Level 3. They get all the facts, but they still tend to miss the vast amount of emotional and contextual information available in every conversation. That's the information you need if you want to achieve Tactical Empathy, and you can only get it by listening at the highest levels.

LEVEL 1: LISTENING INTERMITTENTLY

You're driving your kids to school, and as you explain the logistics of the day, one is staring out the window while the other two poke and gripe at each other. They nod and grunt back at you, but you're not convinced they heard a word you said.

You're on the phone with your dad, and he's telling some dull story about the pests in his garden. You say the right things at the right times ("How annoying! Oh, that's awful."), but afterward, you couldn't retell the story if your life depended on it.

You're in a team meeting, and your boss is going on again about the importance of making a good impression at the convention next week. You've heard it all before, so you try to look attentive while your mind drifts to your dinner plans for tonight.

Listening intermittently is barely listening at all. You may be present, but you are completely checked out. You send superficial signals that you're paying attention—you nod, you say, "Mm-hmm," you make eye contact—but your brain isn't all there. It's trying to focus on two things at once: the person in front of you and the voice in your own head.

That's not unlike the experience of having schizophrenia. When Derek was in law enforcement, negotiators' training included exercises to simulate this so that when they encountered mentally unstable people in the course of their duties, they would have some idea of what those people might be going through. In one exercise, the officer would sit between two coworkers, one of whom talked about pantyhose while the other talked about paper clips. Afterward, what had the trainee learned about pantyhose and paperclips? Absolutely nothing.

In another exercise, the officers were given headphones; in the right ear, a voice with a British accent said disparaging things about them, while in the left ear, a voice with a Spanish accent said negative things about the person in front of them. They had to carry on with their day with both of these voices chattering ceaselessly, making it impossible to focus on the person or task in front of them.

Bottom line: Your brain can only focus on one voice at a time. When you're listening to your inner voice, you can't be fully listening to your counterpart—and it shows. To them, it's obvious you're not paying attention, and that's offensive. You know this from your own experience. When someone isn't really listening, you can immediately tell from their tone and body language, even if they say the right things at the right time. How does that make you feel? Hurt. Disrespected. Irrelevant. Inconsequential. Do you want to listen to the other person? Of course not. You're in fight-or-flight mode; you either want to lash out at them or get away from the conversation entirely.

As you can see, Level 1 listening is dangerous. It doesn't just fail to build trust; it actively damages the relationship. It would be better to not listen at all—to tell your counterpart that you're busy and would rather talk when you can give them your full attention. The next time you catch yourself listening intermittently, pause and make a decision: Either raise your listening game or stop the conversation and come back to it when you're ready to focus.

LEVEL 2: LISTENING TO HIJACK

Your spouse is complaining to you about a coworker who's always driving them up the wall. You sigh and roll your eyes—you've heard it a million times, and to you, the solution is obvious. As soon as they pause for breath, you jump in with your advice.

In a team meeting about an important project, a colleague suggests an approach that you think would be disastrous. Even while they're still talking, you're thinking of all the reasons why their idea wouldn't work. You're just biding your time until they shut up so you can reveal the flaws in their thinking.

A client is chewing you out because your project is running behind schedule. You cut him off and remind him that his team was slow to get you the data you needed, so it's not your fault the work is delayed.

These are examples of listening to hijack: You hear just enough to inform your response, then your focus switches entirely to what you want to say. It's probably fair to say this is the default mode for most people, even when we *think* we're listening closely. We assume that the value we bring to a conversation is in the thoughts we share, so we're eager to express those thoughts. We jump at every opportunity to "contribute" to the discussion.

You might be thinking, *But I'm the quiet type—I prefer not to speak up unless I have to.* Even if you're not outspoken, you probably spend more time than you realize focused on your response to what other people are saying. As they speak, one ear is on them, but the other is on your internal monologue—what *you* think and feel about the words you're hearing. Whether you actually speak them out loud or not, your brain isn't one hundred percent devoted to listening.

This is especially true when emotions are running high. When you're angry, you leap to defend yourself and articulate all the reasons why you're in the right. When you're nervous, you stumble to explain yourself before the other person can attack or judge you. Even when the emotion is a positive one, like excitement, the rush of it keeps you focused on *you*. The physical symptoms of your feelings—elevated heart rate, shallow breathing, tense muscles, et cetera—make it that much harder to pay attention to anything or anyone else.

Listening to hijack is also particularly tempting when you know it will be hard to get airtime. This often happens in group meetings and sometimes in one-on-one conversations with people who really like the sound of their own voice. You know that when you get the chance to speak, you need to make it count. So as soon as you have an idea you want to communicate, you start composing your words and unintentionally tune out everything else.

The obvious danger is that you'll miss important information from your counterpart. Once you start thinking about your response, you probably won't even pick up on the presenting dynamic, let alone the latent one. You might think you're hearing their words, but you're not digesting them; five minutes later, you won't remember what the other person said.

The more subtle and insidious danger is that when you listen to hijack, you can make enemies without even realizing it. As with Level 1 listening, it's obvious to your counterpart that you're not interested in understanding them—you're more concerned with saying your piece. In other words, you don't want to listen to them, but you expect them to listen to you. From their perspective, it's total hypocrisy, not to mention disrespectful. It's easy to see how a person might take offense and get upset or check out of the conversation completely. That's why we always say, if you're explaining too early (as in, before you've made them feel understood), you're losing.

You're probably wondering, *If I don't think about what to say while they're talking, how will I know what to say when they're done?* The answer is simple: Take your time. Don't be afraid to pause. Don't be afraid to speak slowly. Many people mistakenly believe that doing these things will break the flow of the conversation or make them look stupid. The opposite is true, as you'll see later when we discuss Dynamic Silence (chapter 8) and Tone (chapter 11). Time is your friend; use it to your advantage.

For now, our challenge to you is this: *Notice* the next time you're listening to hijack. Your hand will be in the air … you'll be sitting on the edge of your seat … you'll find you can't wait to provide the "right" answer or prove you are right, smart, or talented. It will be more about you than them.

The moment you become aware that you're thinking about what to say back to someone while they're still talking, stop and refocus. If you've ever done yoga or meditation, you know that whenever you notice your mind wandering, you bring it back by refocusing on your breath. With Tactical Empathy, you refocus on curiosity. What's motivating your counterpart's behavior? Asking that question brings your mind back into receiving mode. When the other person is expressing themselves, your *only* task is to receive what they're giving you. As you'll see momentarily, there are way too many layers to that for you to be distracted by your own thoughts.

LEVEL 3: LISTENING FOR INTERNAL LOGIC

You're talking to a potential investor in your start-up who seemed like a sure thing, but he's hesitating at the last minute. From what he says, you can tell he doesn't fully understand your business model but would probably get on board if he saw a more detailed breakdown of it.

Your sister is excitedly telling you about the house she plans to buy. You think it's dicey to choose such a fixer-upper, but it's clear that for her, the big yard and the great location outweigh the risks.

A colleague is asking you to give a last-minute presentation on a topic you're an expert in. It's clear that he thinks it would be no big deal for you to whip something up; he probably has no idea how much thought and effort you put into things like this.

When you're listening for internal logic, you're focused on understanding not just what your counterpart is saying but the *thinking* behind it. What information are they paying attention to? How are they interpreting that information? What assumptions are they making? What's the reasoning that led to the conclusion they're expressing now?

We call it internal logic because it's your counterpart's thinking, which may or may not line up with your own thinking or with reality. This is what separates Level 3 from Levels 1 and 2: In addition to focusing your full attention on the other person, you're also recognizing that the way they think might be different from the way you think. You're actually trying to understand not just the situation but the *person* in front of you.

This is a major step forward. It's the first level at which you might reasonably be considered a good listener; you're actually following the other person's train of thought instead of your own. Ideally, this should be the minimum level at which you engage with another person. It's not the highest level, but the highest levels take so much energy and focus that you can't possibly sustain them indefinitely. At least at Level 3, you're not going to damage relationships the way you do at Levels 1 and 2.

That said, we're still just scratching the surface of the latent dynamic. If Level 3 listening reveals our counterpart's train of thought, we still haven't seen the tracks the train is running on or the landscape it's moving through. We still don't fully understand all the elements that are influencing their mental journey. For that, we have to go deeper.

LEVEL 4: LISTENING FOR EMOTION ATTACHED TO THE LOGIC

Your teenage son is sulking because you won't let him drive the car until his grades improve. You can tell he's mad at you but also disappointed in himself and embarrassed about his grades.

It's your first meeting with a brand-new client, and she's talking fast and asking lots of questions. It seems like she's both excited and nervous to start this project.

You just had to tell an employee that you chose someone else over him for a promotion. You expected him to be disappointed, of course, but from the shock on his face, it's clear that he's blindsided by this news and struggling to process it.

These are examples of listening for the emotion your counterpart has attached to their logic—especially negative emotions. This is crucial because, as we've said before, people are not rational. We do not make decisions based on facts, logic, and reason. We make decisions based on emotion, then justify them with facts, logic, and reason.

Even when you can see someone's internal logic, it may make no sense to you. But as Derek likes to say, everything is logical; you just don't have all the facts. You know what they're thinking, but you still don't know *why*. The why comes down to feelings—not just the surface-level feelings they're saying out loud but also the more nuanced feelings they're not articulating.

For example, let's say you promised to be at your daughter's big soccer game but a client meeting ran over and you showed up late, missing the goal she scored. When you try to congratulate her after the game, she says, "Don't talk to me—I'm mad at you." The logic is, you did not fulfill an obligation. What is the emotion attached to the logic? There's a clear emotion in the presenting dynamic: She's mad. But there are more feelings she didn't say: She feels let down, disappointed, unappreciated, ignored, unimportant ... maybe even unloved.

You can't make her feel understood unless you articulate those emotions back to her, and you can't do that unless you first notice and identify them. Luckily, there's a wealth of information to clue you in: word choice, tone of voice, facial expressions, and body language. In Level 4 listening, you're paying attention to all these factors and making educated guesses about what they mean. Your hypotheses might not always be exactly right—no one is a mind reader—but you might be surprised at how perceptive you can be when you allow yourself to fully receive and process all the information, verbal and nonverbal, your counterpart is giving you.

LEVEL 5: EMPATHETIC LISTENING

Your mother is complaining again that all her children moved so far away. She's been giving you the same guilt trip for decades. It sounds like nagging, but you know she can't let it go because she grew up in a world where three generations lived in the same house and life revolved around family.

A client you've worked with for a long time is up for renewal of their contract, and suddenly they're pushing for a lower price. It's a big company with many vendors and their industry is going through a rough patch, so you suspect your counterpart has orders from higher up to cut vendor costs by a certain amount.

You sit down with your boss for a serious talk about a problematic team member, and your boss is clearly reluctant to take action. You know she's a big believer in second chances; plus, there has been a rash of wrongful termination lawsuits at your company, and she's probably afraid something like that might happen in this case.

As you can see, in these examples we've now gone beyond logic and beyond emotion to *context*. What is the situation your counterpart finds themselves in? What pressures are they under? What do they want? What are they afraid of? What beliefs do they operate on? How does their background, position, or circumstance affect how they're approaching this conversation with you?

Whenever a person's behavior surprises you—when it doesn't seem to line up with the realities of the environment—the reason comes down to context. If emotion explains the why behind a person's internal logic, their context explains the why behind their emotions. Very often, once you understand that context, the behavior starts to make perfect sense.

When you're listening at this level, you're not just paying attention to what's happening in front of you. You're also considering what might be happening in the rest of your counterpart's life, before and after this conversation. The better you know the person, the more information you have to go on, obviously. But even when a relationship is new, you can make a lot of educated guesses about someone's context—and the more you apply the Black Swan skills with them, the more of their context they will voluntarily reveal to you.

Understanding that context allows you to articulate not just their thoughts and emotions but their *worldview*. Worldview is expansive—it's not about one issue but a holistic perspective on life. That's why speaking it out loud is the most powerful way to make someone feel understood and remove yourself as a threat.

The number one reason people fail to articulate their counterpart's worldview is they're afraid that by saying it, they are somehow condoning or approving it. We can't emphasize enough that this is *not* the case. Just because you say what's going through another person's head does *not* mean you agree with it, accept it, or even think it makes sense. You are just acting as a mirror, reflecting back to them what they're showing you.

This is the opposite of the common instinct, which is to criticize and argue with any worldview that differs from your own. In fact, people often think—mistakenly—that it's morally wrong to even *try* to understand a worldview that they find unacceptable. For example, back when Hillary Clinton was secretary of state, she spoke in front of a large audience about the importance of trying to understand the worldview of one's enemies in order to broker peace in armed conflicts. Whether you like her politics or not, from a Tactical Empathy perspective, she was absolutely right. But she caught a huge amount of flak from the public and the media just for suggesting that we should try to see through the eyes of those on the other side of a conflict.

To reiterate one more time: You do *not* have to agree with your counterpart's worldview. All you have to do is speak it out loud, and their guard will start to come down. They will appreciate that you see where they're coming from and aren't jumping to judge or criticize them. Because of that, they'll feel safer in sharing information with you and they'll be far more open to seeing where *you* are coming from. On the flip side, if you don't make the effort to understand and articulate their worldview, their guard will stay up and you'll find it very difficult to have a productive dialogue.

Here's how all this applied in a real situation from my own experience. EOS created a software platform to help our clients implement our coaching. While it was in beta testing, we let clients use it for free, but once it was ready to fully launch, we transitioned to a paid subscription model. One client reacted to this change with a fury that seemed totally out of proportion. The amount of money involved was trivial for his company, so why was he so upset?

A Level 1 listener would ignore this tantrum. A Level 2 listener would immediately explain the logic of the price change. A Level 3 listener would try to follow the client's train of thought, but it wouldn't make sense. A Level 4 listener would identify the underlying emotions driving that train of thought, but the reasons for those emotions would still be unclear. Only Level 5 listening would reveal the full context behind why this small expense was such a big deal.

Maybe he hadn't received the previous communications warning of this coming change, so he felt blindsided by it.

Maybe the company had just decided to freeze its budget and adding this extra cost, even though it was small, would create a major hassle for him.

Maybe he had been in a situation before where small price increases like this one set a precedent for bigger ones in the future and he feared the same thing would happen again.

Maybe he was worried about having to justify this expense to the executive team, since it was his idea to use the software and therefore his reputation on the line.

These were all just insightful guesses based on the totality of what I knew about the situation at the time. To find out which one was right, I had to test my hypotheses (which you'll learn to do in chapter 6). But even before I did that, the act of listening at Level 5 had a very important effect: It put me in a state of *curiosity*.

I could very easily have been triggered by this person's rage and gone into a defensive state. For a moment I did, and if I had responded from that position, I probably would have lost a longtime client or at least damaged our relationship. Instead, I recognized the opportunity to look beyond the surface, and the process of doing so took me out of that defensive state. It allowed me to calm down and make the conversation about him, not me. Because of that, we were able to have a productive dialogue that preserved the relationship and got me what I wanted—his agreement to pay for the software.

HOW TO PRACTICE LEVEL 5 LISTENING

As you can imagine, Level 5 listening is mentally and physically taxing. You're synthesizing a huge amount of information at once—words, tone, facial expressions, and body language, *plus* everything you already know about this person, the world they live in, and the events affecting that world. It's a lot, and you can't keep it up indefinitely. Thirty minutes of it can feel like hours, and by that point, you'll probably want a nap.

That's OK because you don't need to be listening so intensely all the time. On a typical day, listening at Level 3 or 4 is good enough in most of your conversations. However, when "good enough" isn't good enough—when the stakes are high and emotions are running strong—you need to be able to listen at Level 5.

That means you have to practice this kind of listening *before* you really need it. This is the first real Tactical Empathy skill you're learning in this book, the first muscle you need to start strengthening. You already have the cognitive ability to do all the things involved here. You're just not accustomed to doing them all at once during a conversation with another person.

Our advice, which you'll see repeated many times throughout this book, is to start with low-stakes conversations. A pro tennis player doesn't try a new serve technique at the US Open; they perfect it first on the practice courts, where there are no consequences for messing up. So don't start practicing Level 5 listening in sensitive conversations where you're under pressure and likely to be emotionally triggered. You won't succeed, and you'll get discouraged from trying again.

Instead, try choosing one or two low-stakes conversations each day where you intentionally, consciously apply this skill. As you're listening to the other person, deliberately focus on the different layers of information you're receiving. What are they saying out loud? What's their internal logic? What are they feeling? What's the context of it all?

For now, don't worry about doing anything with that information. In part II of this book, you'll learn how to articulate it back to them, but if you focus on that now, your listening will drop back down to Level 2 because you'll be focusing on what to say. For the moment, forget about that and just focus on receiving and synthesizing. If you truly make the effort to parse all the layers of information coming at you, you'll find that there's no room for thinking about yourself. You'll start to feel what it means when we say it's not about you—it's about them.

IN SHORT...

- There are 5 levels of listening:
    - Level 1 is listening intermittently; you have one ear on your counterpart and one on your internal monologue.
    - Level 2 is listening to hijack; you listen only enough to inform your response, then your attention shifts to what *you* want to say when they shut up.
    - Level 3 is listening for internal logic; you try to understand your counterpart's *train of thought*.
    - Level 4 is listening for emotions attached to the logic; you try to decipher the *emotions* driving your counterpart's thinking.
    - Level 5 is empathetic listening; you try to discover the *context* that's creating your counterpart's emotions.

- Levels 1 and 2 will actively damage your relationships. Avoid them at all costs.
- Levels 3 and 4 are a good place to be in everyday, low-stakes conversations.
- Level 5 is too taxing to use all the time, but it's essential for sensitive conversations.
- To be effective at Level 5 listening, intentionally practice it in low-stakes conversations first. This will make it easier to use it in sensitive conversations later.

LOW-STAKES PRACTICE

To start getting comfortable with listening at a higher level, do these exercises.

1. Ask someone the question "What do you love about your job?" Challenge yourself to listen at Level 5: Pay attention to not just the logic of what they're saying but also the emotions attached to that logic *and* the worldview that drives those emotions.
2. Observe a conversation you are not involved in and listen to the two sides as they engage. Listen for latent dynamics missed by one or both sides. What was the impact of missing the latent dynamic?
3. After someone shares something with you, focus on what they did *not* say with the words they used. Paraphrase what your intuition tells you about the latent message behind their words.

**Leverage the Tactical Empathy Logbook at the back of this book to document your practice. When you are ready, share your experience and get real-time feedback from the Black Swan Community.
Scan the QR Code to join.**

CHAPTER 4

THE LAWS OF NEGOTIATION GRAVITY

What is gravity?

Pretty much anybody will tell you that gravity is what makes things fall to the ground and keeps us all from floating off into space.

But *how* does it work?

Those who remember high school physics class might say it works through the force of attraction between objects with mass. The bigger the mass and the smaller the distance between the objects, the stronger the force of attraction.

Yeah ... but *how* does that happen?

The real science junkies will say that according to Einstein's theory of relativity, this happens because mass causes distortions in space-time.

OK ... but *how*?

And here's where it gets crazy: *We don't know.* At the root of it all, we really have no idea how gravity works. We can describe it in precise mathematical detail and use that knowledge to predict how objects will behave in any given situation, but we still don't really know why it happens that way.

The point is this: Just because you don't understand how or why something works doesn't mean you shouldn't believe it. Gravity doesn't care what you believe. If you step off the roof, regardless of your beliefs, gravity will work.

That's why we call the ideas in this chapter the Laws of Negotiation Gravity. We know the 10 claims we're about to make are true because we've seen them in practice over and over again. Some have scientific explanations; others are simply proven by experience. You may find yourself asking why or how they work. Those are perfectly valid and interesting questions—just don't let the lack of an answer get in the way of using this knowledge, because until you accept these 10 truths, you will struggle to make anyone feel understood.

LAW OF NEGOTIATION GRAVITY #1

The fear of loss is the single biggest driver of human decision-making and behavior.

This is the most important law for you to get your head around. *Everything* we do is based on fear at some level. Not the bogeyman-in-the-closet kind of fear—fear of *loss*. Obviously, we fear losing tangible things like people, property, health, and freedom. However, we also fear losing intangible things: love, respect, dignity, reputation, privacy, a sense of safety. Very often, the fear of loss is even stronger for the intangibles than the tangibles.

It's a fact of the human mind that losses overshadow wins. Study after study has shown that the pain of a loss is about twice as strong as the pleasure of an equivalent gain.[*] In other words, if you hit me for $5, I

---

[*] Daniel Kahneman, Amos Tversky, "Prospect Theory: An Analysis of Decision under Risk," *Econometrica*, 47, no. 2 (1979), 263–291.

won't feel like we're even until I hit you back for $10. That's why people move faster and go further to avoid a loss than they do to get a win.

What does this mean for negotiations or sensitive conversations? It means you can't get anywhere until you address the other side's fear of loss.

All too often, you walk into a negotiation ready to pitch gains, benefits, and opportunities. You think that if you provide enough data and logic, you can convince the other side to see what's in it for them. Then when you get pushback, you don't understand why.

It's because your counterpart isn't ready to hear about what they'll win. The whole time you're talking, they're preoccupied with what they have to *lose*. Until that fear is addressed, nothing else matters to them. When you fail to take this into account, you're effectively trying to fix the problem before you understand what the problem really is and what the stakes are for the other person. What are they afraid of losing?

As we said in the last chapter, everything is logical—we just don't have all the facts. The resistance you get from the other side may seem straightforward; they'll object to the obvious things, like price and terms of the deal, but that's never the real issue. That "no" is always covering something deeper, some emotions or context you have yet to identify. Until you address those things, your counterpart will view you as a threat, and your explanations and arguments will fall on deaf ears.

Here's a somewhat unusual example to show you how this law applies in virtually any situation. Derek was on a call with a group of real estate agents who sell units in assisted living facilities to seniors. One agent was complaining bitterly that she "wasted" two hours at a networking dinner with the manager and residents of a senior living facility. The moderator of the call, noticing that the level of rage in the agent's voice seemed out of proportion with the situation, said that it seemed like there was a bigger issue here than just the time.

It turned out that the agent's mother was in an assisted living facility and the agent never spent two whole hours visiting her. How could she justify doing it with other people if she didn't do it with her own mother? Her resistance to that dinner—and future ones like it—wasn't really about the time. It was about fear of losing integrity and respect for herself. Until she recognized that, it would be impossible for her to think clearly about whether to invest her time in networking with potential clients.

As you can see, this law works in both directions. Fear of loss keeps your counterpart in a state of stress and distraction, and it does the same to *you*. If you're too focused on what you're afraid of losing, you won't be able to listen at a high level and you'll miss the signs of what *they* are afraid of losing.

Bottom line: Fear of loss is present in every sensitive conversation, on both sides. Until you address it, both you and your counterpart will be stuck shouting across the street at each other.

LAW OF NEGOTIATION GRAVITY #2

The most dangerous negotiation is the one you don't know you're in.

We said it in chapter 1, and we'll say it here again: A negotiation is any conversation where "I want" or "I need" is in someone's head. It starts in the home and continues through all aspects of life. What's more, it doesn't matter how big the ask is—even the smallest desire can be enough to put both sides on the defensive.

And there's an important point to add to that: If they can see you or hear you, your negotiation has already begun. It doesn't matter if you haven't spoken yet or if you're just exchanging pleasantries and haven't started talking business. You're already exchanging information just through your tone, facial expressions, and body language. You're already laying the groundwork to either build trust or destroy it.

When you don't know you're in a negotiation, it's like taking a knife to a gunfight. You're not prepared, and your expectations are way off. As a result, you stand to lose things you shouldn't—money, opportunity, time, and more.

For example, let's say you're walking into an office to make a sales pitch or interview for a job. That kind of meeting is obviously a negotiation. But before you get to the official meeting, who do you interact with? The receptionist—and that's when the negotiation really begins. That person is a potential deal-killer (more on that in Law of Negotiation Gravity #10), and they might have far more power than you realize. If you're unaware of this, you won't make the effort to use Tactical Empathy and build trust with that person, which may well come back to bite you later. (Remember: Never piss off someone who can hurt you by doing nothing.)

This law even applies when the other side isn't talking back to you. When Derek gets onstage at a live training event, it's a negotiation. He wants his audience's time and attention; they want to learn something that will improve their lives. Those may seem like compatible desires, but the audience may or may not trust Derek and be open to his influence. They may be thinking something like, *What can this ex-cop possibly tell me to help me do my job better? I've been doing this for 30 years. I'm the top performer at my company. What do I need him for?*

If Derek doesn't realize he's in a negotiation, he won't address that resistance and will run the risk of giving his entire presentation to a closed-minded audience. They'll be distracted by their negative emotions, not engaged in what he's teaching. For a speaker, that's the fastest way to bomb. So even though Derek doesn't get to listen to his audience directly, he has to use Tactical Empathy to make them feel understood.

Bottom line: Virtually every human interaction is some kind of negotiation, which means it's an opportunity to get curious and use Tactical Empathy to build trust with your counterpart.

LAW OF NEGOTIATION GRAVITY #3

Your voice will induce emotional reactions
in your counterpart.

This is not the first time we have mentioned this. It will not be the last. The first goal of Tactical Empathy is to remove yourself as a threat. The number one element that will make or break your success is your tone of voice. Tone is one of the first things people use to judge whether or not you are likable, which is directly connected to whether they are going to give you a chance. It registers within one-tenth of a second and is processed at an emotional level, not a cognitive level.

Tone of voice can actually cause a physiological response in your listener. An aggressive tone triggers the release of stress hormones, causing an emotional hijack—a negative reaction that's immediate, overwhelming, and often out of proportion to the actual stimulus. When that happens, the thinking part of the brain shuts down and the limbic system—fight-or-flight mode—takes over. That takes precedence over everything and makes it very hard to think clearly or make good choices. On the flip side, a positive and relaxed tone triggers bonding hormones that make the person feel safe, calm, and open.

You already know this intuitively. If you're a tourist abroad and a stranger starts yelling at you in a foreign language, you will instantly feel attacked even though you have no idea what they're saying. By the same token, you can listen to a guided meditation in that same foreign language and feel soothed without having to understand the words. This is part of our human hardwiring; our mirror neurons tend to mimic the emotions we get from other people, and a crucial vehicle for those emotions is tone of voice. The response is automatic and biological.

And when the tone of voice doesn't seem to match the words coming out of someone's mouth, we're far more likely to believe the tone. In those situations—especially when the topic of conversation is feelings—we base just 7 percent of our conclusions on the person's words, with 38 percent coming from their tone and 55 percent from their body language.* So even if you're saying something positive and agreeable, your counterpart won't believe it if your tone is harsh, impatient, bored, or otherwise negative. If you're not being genuine, tone of voice (along with body language) will betray you every time.

All this says a lot about why text-based conversation is so much less rich than phone, video, or in-person conversation. Without tone of voice, you simply lose too much information. Each person is at liberty to imagine the other person's tone, and whatever they imagine will be based much more on what's going on inside them at the moment than what the speaker intended. If you simply want to inform people, you can use text and email. But if you want to motivate or influence them, you need your voice. (We'll go much deeper on this topic in chapter 11.)

Bottom line: An aggressive tone makes people feel threatened and puts them on the defensive, whereas a friendly tone helps them relax and open up to you.

LAW OF NEGOTIATION GRAVITY #4

*People are six times more likely
to make a deal with someone they like.*

Forget Tactical Empathy—just being nice makes you more influential. Based on no other criteria at all, people prefer to deal with people they genuinely like. They will give more time, attention, information, and money to someone who rubs them the right way than someone who doesn't.

---

* Jessica Stillman, "57 Years Ago, a Legendary Psychologist Discovered the 7-38-55 Rule. It's Still the Secret to Exceptional Emotional Intelligence," *Inc.*, March 29, 2024, https://www.inc.com/jessica-stillman/7-38-55-rule-57-years-old-secret-exceptional-emotional-intelligence.html.

So how do you become likable? Simple: Pay attention to laws 1 through 3. Understand what's at stake for the other person and what they're afraid of losing. Be aware of the fact that whenever somebody wants something from a conversation, it's a negotiation. Use your tone of voice to help remove yourself as a threat. Those three things will go a *long* way.

Last summer, I was putting together a patio chair at my house and I accidentally stripped one of the screws. I really wanted to finish the project, so I raced to the hardware store to get a replacement. I arrived just a few minutes before closing time, keenly aware that all the employees were at the end of a long workday.

When I approached someone to ask for help, I immediately acknowledged what was at stake for him: "You probably just want to get home." That instantly got a warmer response than a straight-up request would have. It also opened the door to some friendly chatting: how long he had worked there, where he lived, et cetera.

Because I was curious about him, he was curious about me in return, so he asked what my screw was for. As soon as I told him it was for a patio chair, he put down the screws he was about to give me and picked up a different box. The first one was galvanized and would have rusted outside—what I needed was stainless steel. And because I was friendly, that's what I got.

Most people think that to be good at negotiation, you can't be too nice; if you are, you'll be a doormat. They think you have to be strong and make the other side bleed to get what you want. *Nothing could be further from the truth.* As we've said before, revenge is a powerful motivator: Make the other side bleed, and they'll work hard to make you bleed too. That combative dynamic is the opposite of what you're trying to achieve with Tactical Empathy. The goal is to build relationships, not destroy them.

And as you'll see later on, being likable and being assertive are *not* mutually exclusive. In fact, Tactical Empathy allows you to be incredibly direct and assertive and to do so without offending your counterpart. This creates an infinitely better experience for both you and the other person than a confrontational approach ever could.

Bottom line: Don't be a jerk. Being friendly and likable gets you much further in any negotiation than being aggressive, pushy, or aloof.

LAW OF NEGOTIATION GRAVITY #5

Your brain works 31 percent more efficiently when it's in a positive state.

This number comes from research by Shawn Achor, author of *The Happiness Advantage*.* He found that if managers intentionally praised their team employees once a day for 21 business days, those teams were 31 percent more productive than the control teams *six months* later. That's some serious impact for just a few positive words. Further studies found that salespeople were 37 percent better at selling and doctors were 19 percent faster and more accurate at diagnosing illnesses when they were in a positive state.

What's going on here? It goes back to what we've said multiple times now: When you're in a negative emotional state, your brain's top priority is protecting you. Your amygdala is activated, making your heart pound and your muscles tighten. Blood flows away from your brain and toward your extremities. That means your prefrontal cortex—your rational mind—just cannot physically operate at full capacity. Your body is prioritizing survival over rational thought.

That's why deactivating the amygdala is so important: It effectively makes you *smarter*. When your negative emotions dissipate, you literally

---

* Shawn Achor, "HBR Idea Cast: Why a Happy Brain Performs Better," accessed February 6, 2025, https://www.shawnachor.com/project/hbr-idea-cast-why-a-happy-brain-performs-better/.

think more clearly, and the same goes for your counterpart. This is crucial because when it comes time for you to deliver information to them or make an ask, you want them in as clear a mental state as possible—not distracted and defensive but attentive and receptive.

You can (and should) apply this logic to yourself as well. *You* want to be in a positive mental state going into a sensitive conversation so you can think clearly and make good decisions. Even more importantly, when your counterpart triggers your negative emotions—which will inevitably happen sometimes—you want to be able to get *back* into a positive state.

Bottom line: It's to your advantage to put yourself and your counterpart in a positive emotional state so you can both think as clearly as possible.

LAW OF NEGOTIATION GRAVITY #6

Labeling positives reinforces them.
Labeling negatives defuses them.

First, a quick definition: Labeling is simply the act of saying out loud what your counterpart is thinking or feeling. It sounds like this: "It sounds / seems / looks / feels like …" and ends with whatever you're observing or surmising about what's going on in their head. You'll learn a lot more about this in chapter 6, but for now that's enough for us to go on.

When you Label something positive, you reinforce it.

- "It seems like you've put a lot of thought into this."
- "It sounds like you're excited to move forward with us."
- "It looks like this decision was an easy one for you."

Your counterpart will appreciate you noticing these things, and hearing you say them out loud makes them feel even more true: *Yes, I* have *put a lot of thought into this. Yes, I am excited to move forward with you. Yes, it was an easy decision.* Reinforcing positives this way also benefits you in that it anchors your counterpart on thoughts and feelings that work in your favor. Because you've reflected those thoughts and feelings back to them out loud, it's much harder for them to later deny those things.

People are usually pretty comfortable with Labeling the positives. Where they get nervous is with Labeling the negatives.

- "It seems like you have some doubts about whether this is the right move."
- "It sounds like you're frustrated with how long this is taking."
- "It looks like you'd like to strangle me right about now."

I know—yikes! You're probably thinking there's no *way* you could ever say that. If they *are* thinking that, won't it just reinforce that thought? And if they're *not* thinking that, won't it make them start?

Surprisingly, no and no. In reality, if they're thinking or feeling something negative, naming it will *defuse* the negativity. Why? Because it shows that you get their perspective, which makes them feel understood. They can see that you're listening; you're open to their viewpoint instead of resisting it, so they no longer have to be on the attack. They can express themselves more calmly.

On the flip side, if they're *not* thinking or feeling something negative, they're not going to start just because you said it. Instead, they will most likely correct you: "No, it's not that at all." Contrary to what your intuition might be telling you, a negative Label will never plant a negative thought that's not already there.

This wisdom comes from the world of suicide prevention—one of the main duties of crisis negotiators like Derek and Chris. The most effective approach is to go right at the issue, not dance around it: "Are you contemplating killing yourself?" There's no need to sugarcoat it. If they weren't already thinking about it, they're not going to suddenly start. If they were, you've instantly made them feel understood and given them a chance to talk openly about it.

What *will* plant a negative thought is *denying* a negative.

- "I don't want you to be upset."
- "Don't take this the wrong way."
- Or, as Richard Nixon famously said, "I am not a crook."

As a listener, your first instinct is to resist. *You don't want me to be upset? Well, maybe I should be.* Or, *You're not a crook? I bet you are.*

Bottom line: All Labels are recognition. Positive or negative, they work in your favor because they make your counterpart feel understood, which is what everyone wants deep down.

LAW OF NEGOTIATION GRAVITY #7

The last impression is the lasting impression.

As the saying goes, "They may forget what you said—but they will never forget how you made them feel."[*]

This is absolutely true. To put it more precisely, in any experience—whether it's one conversation or a monthslong collaboration—people remember the most intense moment and how it ended.[†] If those moments leave a bad taste in their mouth, you're going to have a hard time in any future interactions with them. Conversely, if those moments leave them

---

[*] This saying has been attributed to various people, and its true providence is unclear, but it has been widely repeated, and we believe it's spot-on.

[†] Daniel Kahneman, Barbara L. Fredrickson, Charles A. Schreiber, and Donald A. Redelmeier, "When more pain is preferred to less: Adding a better end," *Psychological Science*, 4 no. 6 (1993), 401–405.

feeling understood and appreciated, you will have gained an ally and advocate.

This has a huge impact on how you handle conflicts and failed negotiations. For example, I recently had a disagreement with a vendor and decided it was time to terminate my contract with them. However, instead of simply canceling the contract and leaving it at that, I got on a call with them to make sure they felt understood and the relationship ended on good terms.

No matter what your field is, you probably operate in a relatively small community—we all do, even in this globally connected world. If you don't think your reputation precedes you, good or bad, you're fooling yourself. Even when you don't come to an agreement with someone, you want them to feel good about you as a person, because this determines whether they'll pick up your future calls and speak well of you to others.

Bottom line: Don't burn bridges. Take the time to leave everyone with a positive feeling about you, even when you decide to part ways.

LAW OF NEGOTIATION GRAVITY #8

The urge to correct is irresistible.

People can't wait to tell you how wrong you are. It makes them feel good—smart, powerful, superior. And here's the fascinating part: They will never correct you with a lie. A correction will always be the truth, and in many cases, it's a truth they wouldn't have shared otherwise.

This allows you to be fearless with your Labels because your Labels don't have to be right. If your Label is right, they'll confirm it and feel understood. If it's wrong, they'll tell you exactly how and why it's wrong—and they'll *still* feel understood because you demonstrated that you're interested in their point of view. You get points just for trying, even when you miss the mark.

You can even use an intentionally incorrect Label—a Mislabel—to draw out more information from your counterpart. Take the story of a young real estate agent who had just signed on with a commercial brokerage. They gave him a lead on a historic building for sale. It was in great shape, with 98 percent occupancy and people lined up to be tenants. He wondered why the owner would want to sell, since the building was practically printing money.

So, the agent used an intentional Mislabel: "It seems like your client doesn't have a strong belief in the fundamentals of the market if he's trying to sell this cash cow."

The listing agent immediately corrected him: "No, it has nothing to do with that. He's underwater on several properties and has to start off-loading them." Oops—the listing agent definitely did not have permission to reveal that, and now this young agent knew the seller was likely to accept a lowball offer.

If you've ever seen the television show *Columbo*, you know exactly what we're talking about. Columbo was a bumbling, unkempt, disarming police detective, and by saying the *wrong* theory out loud, he would often get suspects to inadvertently reveal the truth by correcting him. It's the "aw, shucks" strategy. Because he was nonthreatening and seemingly inept, people let their guard down around him, giving him information they never intended to share.

Bottom line: Don't worry about getting your Labels spot-on. An incorrect Label can be just as effective as a correct one (and sometimes more so) because it prompts your counterpart to give you more information.

LAW OF NEGOTIATION GRAVITY #9

Vision drives decision.

Everyone has a vision of where they want to end up at the conclusion of an interaction. Whatever they've visualized is pushing them in one direction or another, and until you know what that vision is, you won't fully understand what's driving their behavior. So, it's up to you to get that vision out on the table as soon as possible.

That's one of your first steps in any sensitive conversation. In part II of this book, you'll develop a whole collection of tools to get your counterpart talking. But before you make any move to influence them, you've got to get what's in their head out on the table—not just their thoughts, emotions, desires, and fears but also their ideal picture of how this interaction with you will play out.

Getting their vision out in the open does two things for you. First, it helps remove you as a threat. By letting them start with what *they* want, you've shown genuine interest in them and deference to them. That takes them off their guard and sparks their interest in you. Second, it enables you to compare and contrast their vision with yours. It allows you both to clearly see where the gaps are and how you might find a path forward that works for everyone.

Bottom line: Before you can influence your counterpart, you have to understand and articulate their vision of how they want the interaction to turn out.

LAW OF NEGOTIATION GRAVITY #10

There is always a team of deal-killers on the other side.

Many times in a negotiation, you'll get a yes from one person … only to find out later that there are people behind the scenes who are saying no. They might be colleagues, superiors, family members, friends—anybody who might influence your counterpart's thinking, even if they're not direct stakeholders in the issue at hand. You're with your counterpart for a limited time, and then they go back to their own environment, where *someone* is going to sow the seeds of doubt.

The purpose of this law is to stop you from getting happy ears—taking for granted a yes that's not really a final yes. People make this mistake all the time. As soon as they hear what they want to hear, they take their eye off the ball … and then the agreement falls apart. Never forget, the negotiation isn't over until the papers are signed and the money is in the account, literally or figuratively. If you don't make a deliberate effort to address the potential deal-killers, you're likely to wind up disappointed and confused.

So get out in front of it. You don't even have to know who the deal-killer is. Before you let your counterpart go back to their environment, tell them, "There are people on your side who will have a problem with what we discussed. What will you say to them to allay their concerns?" You don't need to tell them what to say or do. Let them decide—that way, they're far more likely to actually do it. (You'll read more on this subject in chapter 17.)

Bottom line: There will always be people behind the scenes who sow doubt in your counterpart about your agreement. To maximize the chances of following through, address that fact before they leave the table.

There you have it: 10 Laws of Negotiation Gravity. There are more, but these are the most important ones. We may not know exactly how or why they work, but they do … whether you believe in them or not. To keep them top of mind, we've got them posted on the wall. It wouldn't be a bad idea for you to do the same.

IN SHORT ...

- There are 10 essential Laws of Negotiation Gravity:
    1. The fear of loss is the single biggest driver of human decision-making and behavior.
    2. The most dangerous negotiation is the one you don't know you're in.
    3. Your voice will induce emotional reactions in your counterpart.
    4. People are six times more likely to make a deal with someone they like.
    5. Your brain works 31 percent more efficiently when it's in a positive state.
    6. Labeling positives reinforces them; Labeling negatives defuses them.
    7. The last impression is the lasting impression.
    8. The urge to correct is irresistible.
    9. Vision drives decision.
    10. There is always a team of deal-killers on the other side.

- Whether you understand why they work or not, these truths drive human behavior. Ignore them at your peril.

LOW-STAKES PRACTICE

To start getting comfortable with the 10 Laws of Negotiation Gravity, print or write them out in a list you can carry with you at all times. Keep it in your wallet or on your phone, where you can find it easily. After every conversation, review the list and make a mental note of the Laws of Negotiation Gravity that were at play in the conversation.

CHAPTER 5

BLACK SWANS

We've mentioned The Black Swan Group a few times already (that's Chris's negotiation training company, in case you forgot). You're probably wondering, *What does a bird have to do with negotiations?*

The answer has a surprisingly long history. The term "black swan" was first used by Juvenal, a second-century Roman satirist and poet, to describe something mythical—something that didn't exist. At the time, no one in Rome had ever seen an actual black swan; the very idea that swans could be any color other than white was ludicrous.

Then, about 1,600 years later, explorers discovered real black swans in Australia. The basic assumption that swans were always white, which everyone had taken for granted, suddenly got debunked. What was once considered impossible was, in fact, the truth. In hindsight, it was easily explained—almost obvious.

More recently, the economist Nassim Nicholas Taleb used the phrase "black swan" to describe seemingly unpredictable events in financial markets, like the dot-com boom or the subprime mortgage crisis. Before they happened, almost no one predicted them or even believed they were possible; they were completely off the radar, like the black swans of Australia. Only in retrospect did we understand how these events came about and gain the ability to predict or prevent them in the future.

For our purposes, a black swan is a piece of information that, if uncovered, changes the dialogue and ultimately the outcome.

A black swan reminds you that you don't know everything and, more importantly, you don't know what you don't know. It forces you to throw out your previous assumptions and recalibrate your understanding of what's really going on. A black swan might be just a small piece of information, but it has a major impact on your perspective.

So why did Chris name his company after this phenomenon? Because sensitive conversations are *full* of black swans.

Every time you enter a conversation, you're going in with an incomplete picture—just like the Romans, who had no idea about the black swans happily paddling about on the opposite side of the planet. You can't possibly know everything there is to know about your counterpart's thoughts, feelings, and circumstances. This is true even when your counterpart isn't intentionally withholding information from you. There's just no way a person (even an honest, trusting, collaborative person) is going to spontaneously reveal every little piece of information that might affect your understanding of the situation. We can't read each other's minds.

You don't know what you don't know ... but you *do* know that you don't have all the pieces of the puzzle. Therefore, your mission in every sensitive conversation is to search for those missing pieces. How does that work when you don't even know what you're looking for? You're about to find out.

FROM WONDERING TO KNOWING

When Derek does live training events, he often asks the participants, "What is a successful negotiation to you?" For many people, success means *winning*. It means getting what they want—or at least getting the most while giving up the least.

That's when he shows them images of two different flying vehicles: the 1917 biplane and the starship *Enterprise* (the famous spaceship of *Star Trek*, in case you're not a sci-fi nerd). Going into a negotiation with the goal of getting what you want is like flying the biplane. It's an antiquated travel method designed for battle. The *Enterprise* is far more advanced, and it's not designed for fighting—it's designed for *discovery*.

Master negotiators don't go into a conversation trying to get the most and give up the least; they're aiming to *discover* what's really going on. A successful negotiation is not necessarily a journey to victory. It's a journey from wondering to knowing. As we emphasized at the very beginning of this book, the skills you're learning here are not foolproof tools for getting exactly what you want. What they *will* get you (if used correctly) is a clear picture of your counterpart's truth.

That's your goal: to find out their truth. The truth of what they want and need. The truth of what they're afraid to lose. The truth of what they're willing or unwilling to do.

When I coach people on using Tactical Empathy in specific situations, they often come back and tell me the skills didn't "work." What this usually means is that the answer they got wasn't the answer they wanted to hear. But they got an answer—and that's what the skills are designed to do. They won't necessarily change what the other person thinks, feels, and wants. They will simply *reveal* those things to you. It's a discovery. The skills get you to the truth of the matter at hand.

You may not like the truth. If you want a yes and the truth is a no, you'll be tempted to keep pushing for your desired outcome. You might get frustrated and think that you're doing something wrong or that the Black Swan skills aren't all they're cracked up to be. The reality is, you simply can't win them all—remember the 7 Percenters we talked about in chapter 2? No trick or skill is going to make someone say yes when the truth is they're not interested in coming to an agreement with you.

That's why your goal isn't to get the answer you want but to get to the truth. Either you find out that you're never going to be able to come to an agreement with your counterpart and it's best to part ways amicably before you waste any more time ... or you reveal a clear path to mutually beneficial collaboration. Either one of those outcomes is a win. The only thing that's not a win is failing to fully understand your counterpart's perspective. If you don't understand their perspective, they won't feel understood, you won't build genuine trust, and you won't be able to discover the best path forward.

And to fully understand your counterpart, you have to uncover their black swans.

We can't emphasize it enough: There's *never* a time when information isn't being hidden. Intentionally or not, your counterpart is omitting important pieces of the puzzle. Those unsaid tidbits can change the outcome in your favor, or at the very least save you time, effort, and stress. So know going in that you don't have the complete picture and it's to your benefit to fill in the gaps.

Black swans never fly alone. In every sensitive conversation, there are probably three to five. That's right—not just one but a handful of small pieces of information that dramatically change the dialogue and the outcome. Once you discover one, you should get excited to investigate further. They might be related to each other, or they might be completely unconnected. As you hear them, it's a good idea to write them down, if at all possible. Think of it like collecting evidence; don't let them go in one ear and out the other.

The key to discovering those black swans is to *stay curious*. Forget about what you think you want. Your goals don't matter right now. Thinking about them won't help you. Your only job is to do two things: *draw out* information from your counterpart and *listen* closely enough to recognize the significance of what they tell you.

It probably sounds crazy to set aside your goals, even temporarily. However, this is absolutely crucial. When you're focused on what you want, your mindset is inflexible. You have tunnel vision—all you can see is the one path in front of you, and you'll stay on it no matter what obstacles get in the way. You see what you want to see (that's confirmation bias). But if you take your blinders off and look around, you might just find there are much easier paths to get to your desired destination—or an even better destination than the one you had in mind. As Derek likes to say, never be so sure about what you want that you wouldn't take something better if it came along.

There's another important benefit to this: When you're genuinely curious, you can't be angry, afraid, or frustrated. Those states of mind are fundamentally incompatible. Negative emotions put you in a defensive mode; when you're experiencing them, your mind is closed off and focused on protecting you from threats. As you learned in chapter 4, this state of mind actually makes you dumber. You don't think as clearly or make the best decisions when you feel threatened.

Curiosity is the complete opposite. It's a state of openness, where you're calm, clearheaded, and receptive to new information. That's the frame of mind you want to be in during any negotiation … and focusing on discovering black swans will help you stay there.

RECOGNIZING THE BLACK SWANS

You just learned that discovering black swans requires that you get your counterpart talking and listen closely to what they say. You've already learned what it means to listen like a master negotiator, and in future chapters, you're going to learn lots of specific skills to help you draw information out of people. But before we go there, we want to make sure you understand what a black swan is and how to recognize one when it's revealed to you. So, let's look at some real-life examples.

Example: Misunderstood Procurement Professionals

At one Black Swan training event, there was a discussion around procurement, a job where negotiation is center stage every day. Many of the participants brought up horror stories of negotiating with procurement people: how they made impossible demands, haggled endlessly, dragged their feet, changed their minds, and ghosted their counterparts. The coaches—including Derek—were going hard on procurement professionals, pointing out the flaws in their traditional approach to negotiation.

It turned out there were a few procurement people in the audience, and one stood up, almost in tears. She said everyone had such a narrow view of who the people in her profession really were. No one understood what they were going through every day. "It's like herding cats in a house that's on fire while the villagers are out front with pitchforks," she said.

That was a black swan. No one in the room—whether coaches or audience members—was appreciating that procurement people are in a vise and the pressure is sometimes overwhelming. When they're beating you up over price, they're not trying to be obnoxious or offensive. They're doing what they've been hired to do—what they're *required* to do to avoid losing their jobs (notice how fear of loss comes into play).

This knowledge completely changes your understanding of their behavior in a negotiation. When they're making seemingly unreasonable demands, instead of getting upset and coming to the conclusion that they're a jerk or they don't respect you, you can stay calm and try to figure out exactly who is putting pressure on them and what it would take for them to satisfy those people.

Example: A Bad Quarter

At a recent training event, one of the participants told us about a negotiation he had been having with Amazon. The conversation had been in progress for about a month, and it seemed like they were about to close the deal. Then, at the last minute, Amazon came back and wanted to pay less than what they had already agreed to.

After some patient digging, our negotiator learned that Amazon had just closed a bad quarter and it was trying to cut costs by taking a piece out of each of its vendors. That completely changed his approach to the conversation. Instead of fighting with the Amazon rep over price, he could say, "I know you've been pressured to bring vendor costs down across the board. This is not what you want to hear. Our contract is relatively small, and we can't cut the price any further without undermining our ability to provide the services you need. Would it be out of the question to honor our agreed price and find those savings with another vendor who has more wiggle room?"

By showing that he understood the rep's perspective, our negotiator built such strong rapport that the rep felt like they were friends by the end of the negotiation process. He avoided a $500,000 cut to the contract, and he now has a strong ally for future negotiations—one who appreciates his value and is far less likely to squeeze him on price.

Example: Ghosted or Not?

A while back, a prospective client reached out to me, seemingly interested in working together. After our first conversation, he disappeared. I have a very strong rule against chasing business—the last thing I want to do is waste time pursuing someone who is never going to hire me. I wanted to get to the truth as quickly as possible: Was he or was he not interested in moving forward?

So, I reached out one more time (using a highly effective question you'll learn about in chapter 18). I got an immediate response containing a very important black swan: His company was in the middle of a major fundraising effort, and everything else was on hold until that was done. He wasn't ghosting me; he was just overwhelmingly busy at the moment. Now I knew exactly what to do: wait and reach back out in a month, when he would have time to give our conversation his full attention. In the end, the deal closed—just not on my original timeline.

Looking for black swans is like hunting for truffles. We're trying to dig up little pieces of extremely valuable information that explain the other person's behavior, especially when they're behaving in a way that seems inappropriate, confusing, or unfair. These tidbits may have nothing to do with the matter at hand, but they have everything to do with how your counterpart is feeling during your conversation.

For example, let's say you're in a business negotiation where the other side is pushing back hard on price. That's the behavior, but what's motivating it? Maybe she's up for a promotion, everyone is watching her, and this deal may determine whether she gets the job. Maybe she just put in an offer on a home, and if this deal doesn't go through, she won't have enough money for the closing. Maybe she's in discussions with other vendors, and you're not actually her top choice. Maybe she's remembering a past deal where she overpaid and regretted it later.

These are all potential black swans that you will not uncover unless you allow the conversation to expand beyond the narrow scope of the deal at hand. Very often, your counterpart is *hoping*, consciously or unconsciously, that you will discover and recognize these crucial facts. Often when you uncover a black swan and articulate it back to them, they immediately become more collaborative. As we've said before, every human desperately craves being understood.

MAKE IT A GAME

So, in your hunt for black swans, ask yourself ...

What kind of pressure are they under? Internal deadlines? Budgets? Performance expectations? Do they have something to prove?

What's their psychological state, and why? What's going on in their personal life? What's going on at work? What have they already been through today?

What has happened to them in past situations like this one? What assumptions might they be making about you and your motives?

What else have you missed that might explain what you're seeing?

Our best advice is this: Make it a game. Challenge yourself to see how many black swans you can find. Tally them up, like notches in your belt. When you find one, don't stop looking. As mentioned, there are almost always more, and they may or may not be related to each other.

This puts you in the ideal frame of mind for any sensitive conversation. You're calm, curious, and focused on the other person, which maximizes your chances of achieving the ultimate goal: getting to the truth.

When you discover a black swan, acknowledge it out loud (you'll learn more about exactly how to do this in the next few chapters). Let your counterpart know that you heard them and you recognize the importance of what they've told you. Do this even if the black swan is something that doesn't work in your favor—something you didn't want to hear. Whether you like it or not, it's the truth, and failing to acknowledge it won't change that.

Most importantly, be careful of impatience. We're all conditioned to want instant gratification, but don't fall for that trap. As we've said before, Tactical Empathy is all about slowing down to speed up—taking the time to understand your counterpart and build trust so you can collaborate more easily over the long term.

Searching for black swans takes time. To find them, you must allow the conversation to expand. You must encourage your counterpart to talk about things that may seem irrelevant—their work situation, their personal life, their past experiences, and more. If you rush, you'll miss the opportunity to discover valuable information that can work in your favor, if only by getting you to the truth faster.

IN SHORT ...

- A black swan is a piece of information—big or small—that dramatically changes the dialogue and, by extension, the outcome of a sensitive conversation.
- People are *always* hiding information, intentionally or unintentionally.
- Your goal in every negotiation is to get to the *truth*—the truth of what your counterpart wants, what they're afraid to lose, and what they're willing or unwilling to do.
- To do that, you have to discover their black swans. These are the missing pieces to the puzzle of why they're behaving the way they are, and there are at least three to five of them in every sensitive conversation.
- Discovering black swans requires you to *stay curious*, even when you think you know what's going on. Make it a game—see how many you can find.

LOW-STAKES PRACTICE

To start learning how to listen for black swans, do these exercises.

1. **Look for contradictions.** Practice observing when someone's words and actions don't align (e.g., they say they're excited about a project but seem disengaged). Note these contradictions and explore them gently.
2. **Don't take the first rejection at face value.** When someone says no or seems hesitant, their resistance is often camouflaging something else. What is behind the no?
3. **Notice the effect of genuine curiosity.** When talking to a stranger or acquaintance, make a point of demonstrating sincere interest without judgment of their circumstances, environment, or demeanor. Observe how that impacts their level of engagement. Document the black swans delivered.

Black Swans don't shout—they whisper. Spotting them takes presence, practice, and pattern recognition. Scan the QR code to join the Black Swan Community, where others are comparing notes and uncovering the unexpected right alongside.

PART II

THE CORE FOUR

There are lots of tools in the Tactical Empathy toolbox, but these four skills are your bread and butter. You can use them with anyone, in any situation, and see a huge difference in how they respond to you. That said, these "basic" skills aren't necessarily easy; they are counterintuitive, and it takes practice to master them. Here's what you're about to learn:

- How to Label what your counterpart is thinking and feeling
- How to Mirror them to draw out more information
- How to use Dynamic Silence to give them space to think and express themselves
- How to use Summaries to get on the same page

CHAPTER 6

LABELS

As a business strategy coach, I often facilitate intensive, all-day planning sessions with company leadership teams. We start the day by going around the table and checking in with each person. The check-in involves five questions:

- What's the best thing happening in your personal life?
- What's the best thing happening in your professional life?
- What's working for you in your role right now?
- What's not working for you?
- What are your expectations for today?

I was in a session with a relatively new client; this was only their second session with me, the first one having been about a month prior. The first person to do the check-in was the strategic leader of the team. He was feeling optimistic and brave, and he answered each of the five questions with enthusiasm.

Next up was a technical member of the team. I asked, "What's the best thing happening in your personal life?"

He scowled in silence for a moment, then said, "I got nothing."

"Nothing?"

"Nope."

I waited for a moment to see if he would change his mind, but no luck. So, I moved onto the next question.

Again, nothing.

Nothing, nothing, nothing. Not one thing to share for any of the five questions.

I thought to myself, *Houston, we have a problem.*

I didn't react or respond to his obstinance yet, though. First, we had to respect the process and finish the check-in with the rest of the team. The other four members checked in as expected—no stony silence, no evasion, no surliness. So, we were five for six on team health … but I knew from experience that anything less than one hundred percent buy-in was a losing formula. Even if just one member of the leadership team was not on board, this was not going to work.

So, what to do? This guy obviously had an issue he was reluctant to share. How could I get it out on the table so we could address it as a team? Effectively addressing such challenges is what you'll learn in this chapter. We'll tackle one of the most fundamental tools in your Tactical Empathy arsenal: Labels. This one skill by itself can get your counterpart talking *and* go a long way toward making them feel understood.

WHAT IS A LABEL?

A Label is a verbal observation of your counterpart's emotions, desires, fears, motivations, circumstances, or dynamics.

We introduced this concept briefly in chapter 4, but we're about to go much deeper. When you use a Label, you're gathering data with your senses, then demonstrating your receipt of that data by expressing it out loud. This accomplishes two things. First, it makes your counterpart feel understood because it proves that you heard their words, noticed their nonverbal signals, and recognized their significance. Second, it encourages them to provide more information. If your Label is right, they will confirm it and possibly expand on it, and if it's not right, they will correct you.

A Label has a very specific structure:

> "It sounds/looks/seems/feels like …"
> or
> "You probably feel/think/want …"

As you can see, these two structures are very similar. The only difference is the choice of "it" or "you" to start the sentence. "It" is neutral; "you" is a bit more personal and direct. For example: "It seems like you're upset" versus "You seem upset." The distinction is subtle, but it can make a difference in how the Label lands. As you practice using Labels, you'll start to get a sense of which choice feels right given the context.

A Label is a powerful tool, and it will probably be the one you reach for most often. Here's what you need to know to use it successfully.

Labeling the Presenting Versus Latent Dynamic

In chapter 2, we introduced the concept of presenting and latent dynamics. Here's a quick refresher: The presenting dynamic is what your counterpart is literally saying or showing. The latent dynamic is what's under the surface—the emotions, desires, fears, and motivations they *haven't* explicitly articulated.

Labeling the presenting dynamic is easy … but not nearly as effective as Labeling the latent dynamic. To see why, put yourself in the shoes of the person being Labeled.

You're yelling at me for being late *again*, and I say, "It sounds like you're angry that I'm late."

You've just explained that you need this task done immediately, and I say, "You probably want this done quickly."

You're sobbing, and I say, "It seems like you're upset."

What's your first thought? *Duh. No shit, Sherlock.* Do you feel understood? Nope. Do you feel the urge to tell me more about your thoughts and feelings? Nope.

Now, let's see what happens when I Label the latent dynamic instead.

- "It sounds like you're angry that I'm late." ➜
  "It feels like I've smacked you in the face by not showing up at the agreed time."
- "You probably want this done quickly." ➜
  "It sounds like you're under a lot of pressure to keep this project on schedule."
- "It seems like you're upset." ➜
  "It looks like something horrible must have happened just now."

Do you feel the difference? I'm going *beyond* what you actually said. I'm making an educated guess about what's beneath the surface—what you're thinking and feeling but didn't say out loud. That guess is based on everything I'm getting from you—your words, your tone, your body language, and anything else I already know about you. My intuition is picking up all those signals and connecting the dots so I can articulate the things you haven't said but want me to know.

That's what it means to Label the latent dynamic. Labeling the presenting dynamic shows that I heard what you said, but Labeling the latent dynamic shows that I truly see your perspective. There's no clearer way for me to demonstrate that I'm locked in and paying attention to you.

That makes you feel understood, which makes you feel calmer, more trusting, and more open to both sharing and receiving information.

People who are new to the Black Swan skills are often amazed at how directly we go after the latent dynamic. They think, *I can't just say that. I don't know if it's right! What if I offend them?* As you're about to learn in the next section, there's nothing wrong with being wrong. There's no penalty for trying.

However, there often is a penalty for *not* trying. It's OK to start out with Labeling the presenting dynamic, especially when you're first learning this skill. But if you're not going deep enough, your counterpart will let you know; they will get frustrated, or withdraw, or send some other signal that you need to go beyond the obvious. If you fail to heed those signals, you can forget about influencing them. They're going to feel like you're listening but not really *getting* it. They're lobbing you softballs, and you're not swinging.

So, trust what your intuition is telling you. Look beyond what's right in front of your face, and have the courage to say it out loud. Labeling the latent dynamic will always be more powerful than Labeling the presenting dynamic.

Mislabeling

That brings up an important question: What if you aren't sure what the latent dynamic is?

Make an educated guess. If you're wrong, your counterpart will feel an irresistible urge to correct you (remember Law of Negotiation Gravity #8). That's human nature—we *love* to tell people they're wrong. So if your Label is off base, your counterpart will tell you exactly why, which is a win for you because your goal is to get to the truth. And despite what you might expect, your counterpart will not fault you for Mislabeling the situation. On the contrary, they'll still feel more understood than before because you gave them an opportunity to express something important.

This is the beauty of Labels—you get credit for trying, whether your Label is right or wrong. (So to all the perfectionists out there, no excuses!)

In fact, you can strategically use intentional Mislabels to draw more information out of your counterpart. The urge to correct is so strong that it may lead them to reveal things they otherwise wouldn't have shared, especially the true motivations behind their actions. Be careful here—you don't want to overuse this tactic, and you don't want your Mislabel to be so wrong that it's ridiculous. That said, a judicious Mislabel can be a very helpful tool in getting to the truth.

Occasionally, a Mislabel may trigger a negative reaction from your counterpart, especially if they're already in a negative emotional state. You test an assumption about what they're thinking, and they respond with something like, "No, dummy, that's not it at all!"

The most effective response is this: "I'm sorry. I didn't say you *were* _____ . I said it *seems* like you're _____ . How is what I'm hearing/seeing wrong?"

You're doing three things here. First, you're apologizing. Then, you're pointing out that your statement was simply an observation of what you're seeing or hearing (this is where the specific structure of Labels comes to the rescue). Then you're asking them to correct you or fill in the blanks. This takes the focus off you and puts it back on them, and it encourages them to move the conversation toward the truth—which is always the ultimate goal.

Labeling Negatives and Positives

Don't forget Law of Negotiation Gravity #6: Labeling positives reinforces them; Labeling negatives defuses them.

Labels are rarely emotionally neutral. Usually, the dynamic you're Labeling can be considered negative or positive to some degree. Instinctively, most people are very comfortable Labeling positive dynamics and not so comfortable Labeling negative dynamics. So they do too much of the former and not enough of the latter. Unfortunately, that's the *opposite* of what you need to do.

Labeling negative emotions and fears reduces their power. By acknowledging them explicitly, you make the other person feel understood, which immediately reduces their stress levels. Their negative emotions can begin to dissipate, and they can start to think more clearly; you might be surprised at how quickly this happens. Plus, by bringing the negatives out into the open, you make it possible to examine, discuss, and resolve them.

That's why it's extremely important to *always* Label negative dynamics as soon as you become aware of them. It might feel scary to you, especially at first, but it goes a *long* way toward building trust and making progress with your counterpart. Any negative dynamic that goes unacknowledged is an obstacle in your conversation. As we've mentioned before, unexpressed emotions never die—they always come back to bite you.

On the other hand, Labeling the positives is more of a self-serving move. It either strengthens your position or strokes your counterpart's ego, making it more likely that they'll do what you're hoping for.

- "It sounds like you haven't found anyone else who can match what we're offering."
- "It seems like you're excited to work on this project together."
- "It looks like you've become a real expert on this subject."

Labeling the positives is an important step, especially in a Proof of Life conversation (more on that in chapter 16), but be careful. If you do it insincerely or too much, it can easily come off as fake and manipulative; people can smell intent.[*] If you're listening too hard for positives to Label, you're likely to gloss over or dismiss the negatives that need to be called

---

[*] Dare A. Baldwin and Jodie A. Baird, "Discerning Intentions in Dynamic Human Action," *Trends in Cognitive Sciences* 5, no. 4 (2001): 171–178, https://www.sciencedirect.com/science/article/abs/pii/S1364661300016156.

out. That's a big danger because if you don't Label the negatives, they'll stick around and cloud your counterpart's mind, which keeps them closed off to your influence.

WHEN TO USE LABELS

In any sensitive conversation, there are many moments when you can use a Label.

1. When your counterpart has given you important information.
This is a perfect opportunity to make them feel understood by showing you're paying attention. Remember, the deeper you go beyond the surface, the more effective your Label will be.

- Example: You're talking to a prospective client, and they've just finished telling you how their current vendor isn't reliable.
    "It sounds like you're looking for someone who will always deliver on their promises."

- Example: Your partner has just spent five straight minutes complaining about her boss's constant micromanagement.
    "It seems like you're infuriated that your boss doesn't trust your competence."

2. When you want to ask a question or get more information.
When you're trying to gather information, your instinct is to ask questions. However, direct questions—no matter how innocuous—can often feel invasive or threatening. That puts your counterpart on the defensive and makes it harder to get them talking.

To see what we mean, just imagine yourself at a cocktail party, surrounded by people you don't know. A friendly looking guy comes up and introduces himself, then asks, "So, what do you do?" You sigh inside. Where do you even begin? This person doesn't know you at all; they don't actually care. So you just say, "I'm in finance."

Or imagine a teenage girl coming home from school. As soon as she walks in the door, Dad hits her with, "How was your day?" Eye roll. "Fine," she says. She's not going to take the time to explain that she nailed her solo in band rehearsal but she bombed her chemistry test and her two best friends are fighting over a boy. Dad doesn't need to know.

Turning the question into a Label can get you the same information with less pressure on your counterpart. Their response is more likely to be spontaneous and therefore more candid. For example:

- "Why do you want this?" ➜
  "It sounds like you have a reason for wanting this."
- "What are you going to do?" ➜
  "It seems like you have a vision for what comes next."
  (You'll see this Label again in chapter 16.)
- "How do you feel about this?" ➜
  "It sounds like you have strong feelings about this."
- "How was your day?" ➜
  "It seems like you've had one hell of a day."

Labels like these won't make them feel like you're putting them on the spot, as they might have if you had asked the direct question.

3. When you want to test a hypothesis about your counterpart's perspective.

Very often in a sensitive conversation, the other person doesn't explicitly say what they really feel, think, or want. However, by gathering the data with your eyes and ears (as you learned in chapter 3), you will glean all kinds of clues from their tone and body language. You might even uncover black swans related to their history and their current circumstances.

That's plenty of information to come up with a theory of what's going on under the surface.

But the only way to know if your theory is right is to say it out loud. Once again, they will either confirm it or correct it, and it's a win for you either way.

- Example: You sent a contract to a prospective client who seemed excited to get started, but they're taking unusually long to sign it.

    "It seems like you're having second thoughts about working together."

- Example: Your teenage daughter is giving you the silent treatment, and you don't know why.

    "It seems like I did something to offend you."

- Example: You walk up to the check-in desk at your hotel, and the concierge gives you a curt greeting while furiously typing on the computer.

    "Looks like you're in an arm-wrestling match with the system."

Given what you know in each of these situations, these seem like plausible explanations for the other person's behavior. However, you won't know if you're right until you say it out loud. In doing so, you go from wondering to knowing and you start to make your counterpart feel understood.

4. When you notice an emotional shift in your counterpart.
A wrinkled brow. A huff of laughter. Crossed arms. Wandering eyes. The other person can say a *lot* without saying anything at all … and this presents a golden opportunity to demonstrate that you are completely dialed in. Anytime you notice a change in your counterpart's affect, even

a small one, Label it. This shows that you're paying close attention to them (which, as you know, helps make them feel understood) and invites them to explain what they're feeling and why.

- Example: You're reviewing the contract terms with a client, and when you get to point number five, she frowns.
  "It looks like you have some reservations about this point."

- Example: You're with a renovation contractor in your kitchen, and when you explain your vision, he steps back and crosses his arms.
  "It seems like you might have had some challenges with a similar kitchen layout in the past."

- Example: You're giving a presentation to your project team at work, and when you get to slide 23, one person shakes her head and looks away.
  "It seems like you think this slide is a dumpster fire."

Once again, you're testing a hypothesis about why this person's body language changed. Maybe your hypothesis is wrong. Maybe that client frowned because she was confused by the wording of point number five. Maybe your contractor crossed his arms because a cold breeze blew through the kitchen. Maybe your colleague shook her head because the meeting is running long and she can't believe you still have more slides to get through.

The only way to get to the truth—your ultimate goal—is to Label what you're seeing and let your counterpart respond.

5. When you want to show appreciation for your counterpart.
For most people, the default way to express appreciation is with praise: "Great job! This is so thoughtful/useful/creative/impressive." That's not

bad, but with a Label, you can do better. A well-crafted positive Label shows appreciation not just for what the person did but for who they are and how they did it. It makes the person feel appreciated in a way that simple praise doesn't.

- Example: Your kid just gave you a handmade gift for your birthday.

    "It seems like you put a lot of thought and love into this."

- Example: Your team just handed in the final draft of an important report just under the deadline.

    "It looks like you guys pulled some seriously late nights to get this done on time."

- Example: A loyal client pushed a contract renewal through despite his team's concerns about your price increase.

    "It sounds like some very artful diplomacy was undertaken to get this done."

In these situations, the best Labels emphasize what the *other person* values—not what you care about but what *they* crave to be recognized for. Knowing their Negotiator Personality Type (which you'll learn about in chapter 15) helps a lot with this. However, even if you don't know their type, you can use whatever you do know about them to make an educated guess about what would make them feel seen.

THE PITFALLS OF LABELING

Labels are simple in theory but surprisingly easy to screw up in practice. Here's what *not* to do.

1. Don't start with "I."

A Label is *not* an "I" statement. As always with Tactical Empathy, the goal is to keep the focus on the other person, not yourself. Therefore, you should *never* use phrases like the following:

- "What I hear you saying is …"
- "I get the sense that you …"
- "I see that you …"
- "I understand that you …"

Note that we're not saying you should never use "I" anywhere in a Label sentence. If you need to Label how the other person feels about you (e.g., "You probably think I'm the worst partner ever"), you definitely need the word "I." What we're saying is that "I" should never be the *subject* of the sentence.

Note: There is one important exception to this rule. If the dynamic you're Labeling is something they've expressed in a clear, unmistakable way, it is appropriate to start a Label with "I know you feel/think/want …"

For example, when Derek spoke to the families of hostages, he *knew* they were devastated. There was no question about it. So he would say, "I know you're devastated right now."

If he used a weaker Label like, "It seems like you're concerned about your family member," how do you think those parents would respond? With something like, "*Concerned?* My son is being held hostage! *Of course* I'm concerned!" They wouldn't feel understood at all—they would think their hostage negotiator was an oblivious idiot.

When your kid is ranting in a rage in front of you, you *know* they're angry. When a client has told you they have a tight deadline to meet, you *know* they want to move fast. When a colleague has called you a bully to your face, you *know* they think you've crossed the line. Such clear and strong messages must be met with an equally clear and strong Label: "I know you feel/think/want …"

2. Don't step on your Label.

Probably the most common mistake people make with a Label is undermining it after they say it. A Label only works if you give it space to land and give your counterpart time to respond to it. Here's how to do that.

Label ONE thing, then shut up.

One emotion, one thought, one dynamic. Short and sweet, usually no more than ten words. Then, Dynamic Silence (more on that in chapter 8). We can't emphasize it enough: Your counterpart needs time to process what you've said and, if they are moved to, respond to it.

Do NOT follow your Label with "but."

"But" is an erasing word—it negates everything that comes before it. To understand what we mean, let's see it in action.

First, consider a Label without a "but:" "I know you despise me for this."

Let's imagine your counterpart *does* despise you for this (whatever "this" is). You saying so might not change that, but it does make them feel seen, and it gives them an opportunity to further express their feelings and the reasons behind them. They might respond with something like, "Yeah, what you did was really shitty, especially because you did it before and promised it would never happen again."

If your counterpart *doesn't* despise you, they'll say so and tell you what they really feel. "I don't despise you—I'm just disappointed." Great! Now you're closer to the truth, and you can use this clue to dig even deeper.

Now, let's look at the same Label followed by a "but": "I know you despise me for this, but it's for your own good."

What would be *your* first reaction if someone said that to you? Probably something along the lines of, "F*ck you! Who are you to decide what's for my own good and what's not!" You don't feel understood—you feel enraged. You don't want to explain how you really feel—you want to bar the gates and start shooting volleys from the ramparts. The first half of the sentence might as well not be there.

It doesn't matter what comes after the "but"—any way of ending that sentence would have the same effect. See for yourself:

- "I know you despise me for this, **but** I never meant for it to happen this way."
- "I know you despise me for this, **but** it's for the best in the long run."
- "I know you despise me for this, **but** I can fix it."

No matter what follows the "but," the Label disappears and your counterpart is left in a defensive position—the opposite of what you want. "But" is the mortal enemy of every Label. It's better not to Label at all than to step on a Label with a "but" statement.

Do NOT follow your Label with "and."
Just like "but," the word "and" will kill your Label. Whether you use it to string multiple Labels together or to tack something else onto your Label (a suggestion, a promise, an opinion, etc.), it completely negates the power of the Label to make your counterpart feel understood and invite them to share more information. For example:

- "It seems like you're uncomfortable with this process **and** would prefer to do it a different way."
- "I know you're thinking I'm the worst teammate ever **and** have no idea what I'm doing **and** should never have been brought on the team in the first place."
- "It sounds like you're looking for a better option, **and** I can help you with that."
- "It feels like we're on the right path, **and** the next steps are pretty clear."

These might not be quite as catastrophic as the "but" examples, but they are all major missed opportunities to build trust and get more information.

The first two are multiple Labels strung together. People often do this when they're nervous about how the other side will respond; you're afraid to find out how they really feel, so you keep talking to put off the moment of truth. The problem is that when the other person has to process more than one thing, they will most likely only respond to the last one in the list—and if you really overload them, they might not respond constructively at all. It's always better to deliver each Label one at a time, followed by enough silence that the other person can digest and respond.

The last two examples are Labels followed by something else. Again, your counterpart will probably only respond to the last thing they hear. You're not going to find out whether they're really looking for a better option and what that means to them. You're not going to find out if they agree that you're on the right path or what they're thinking and feeling about that. Their opportunity to share got crushed by your suggestions and opinions. Because of that, they don't feel understood and you don't get any closer to the truth.

Do NOT follow your Label with "because."
You're probably sensing a theme here. "Because" is another word that undermines your Labels. It is you succumbing to the inclination to explain why you Labeled what you did. For example:

- "I know you're wondering if I'm a serious prospect **because** I haven't responded to your emails in a week."
- "It seems like you're worried about setting the price too low **because** that might leave money on the table."
- "It sounds like you think I should make an exception to the rules **because** this is a special circumstance."

This is no different from the "and" situation. By trying to explain the Label, you're attempting to alleviate your own discomfort by showing you have reasons for saying what you said. Don't do it. All of these Labels work much better if you stop before the "because" and forget about the rest.

Rule of thumb: If you feel yourself wanting to use *but*, *and*, or *because*, replace those words with Dynamic Silence.

3. Don't use a Label to attack or judge.
Like any of the Black Swan skills, Labels can be used for good or evil. One of the hardest things about Labels—especially when you're triggered—is resisting the temptation to use one to drive home a point or smack the other person down.

This is nuanced. There are no hard-and-fast rules about what words to use or avoid. Whether a Label feels like an attack or not ultimately comes down to the context, the other person's state of mind, and your tone and body language when you deliver the Label.

- Example: *"It sounds like you're inexperienced with these kinds of situations."*

This might not be so bad if your counterpart is a novice who has come to you for expert advice and has been very up front about being a newbie who has no idea what he's doing. However, you can probably imagine plenty of situations where someone would not appreciate being called out for their lack of experience. This can easily come off as dismissive, disdainful, and insulting. A better way to phrase this would be *"It sounds like you haven't faced circumstances like this before."*

If you're in a negative frame of mind about the other person and you can imagine how good the words are going to taste when they roll off of your tongue, you probably shouldn't say them. If your Label is designed to make the other side feel bad, it's the wrong one to use. Take a deep breath, set aside the urge to take a swing, and focus on switching your frame of mind from self-defense to curiosity.

4. Don't overdo it.
A funny thing often happens during Black Swan role-play exercises: People get so focused on Labeling each other that they forget to have a real conversation. Instead of a productive dialogue, it becomes a war of the Labels. Just like in the card game War, each side just keeps throwing down cards; no one is really listening to each other or getting any closer to the truth.

Labels, like all the Black Swan skills, are like seasoning. They're what makes a dish delicious instead of bland, but overusing them will make the food inedible. If you respond with a Label to everything your counterpart says, the conversation will start to feel unnatural and insincere.

There's no strict rule about how much is too much. We're not going to tell you that you can have a maximum of one Label per minute or no more than three Labels in a row. Again, this is nuanced. It comes down to your intuitive judgment as a human being who has spent a lifetime talking to other human beings. Listen to yourself. If you sound forced, fake, or annoying, you can bet your counterpart has noticed it too, which makes them less likely to trust and open up to you.

When in doubt—as with any seasoning—it's better to underdo it than overdo it. You can always add more later.

CASE STUDY RESOLUTION

Now that you know all about Labels, let's go back to my story about the strategy session check-in gone wrong.

Where we left off, one member of my client's team of six had just refused to respond to the check-in questions. After we finished checking in with the rest of the team, I did a little debrief. I got up and pointed to the board on the wall that showed the three pillars of my coaching philosophy, one of which is Team Health—how well the team is functioning, as individuals and as a whole.

I said to the group, "Seventy percent of the success of this process is rooted in Team Health." Then I looked the disgruntled team member straight in the eyes and used a Label: "It seems like there's a reason you're unwilling to share anything with the team."

And I waited …

And waited …

And waited some more …

Finally he said, "Well, I don't trust some people on this team."

Trust is an issue that comes up a lot in these sessions—so much that I have a go-to video clip of Simon Sinek talking about the importance of trust, which I use precisely for occasions like this. I played the video. When it was over, I reminded everyone, "Remember, in these sessions, we speak our truth and we use explicit names."

He said, "I am unwilling to share names … but I am not sure that I belong on this team."

I went to the board again and wrote "GWC." It was a reminder of something we had discussed in detail in the previous session, a tool for determining whether someone in the company is in the right seat. It stands for Get It (Do they understand the role?), Want It (Do they want the role?), and Capacity (Are they capable of fulfilling the role?).

I looked at him again and used another Label: "It feels like you don't want your seat."

He pondered this for a while and eventually said, "No, I don't want the seat."

He stood up, grabbed his bags, and walked out.

That might not seem like a happy ending, but in fact it was. We got to the truth, and we did it fast, with minimal drama. If not for that conversation—and the power of a couple choice Labels—who knows how much longer that unhappy team member would have stuck around and how much damage he might have done in the process. After he left, a sense of levity came over the room, and the team gladly agreed to focus on the future for the rest of the session.

IN SHORT ...

- A Label is a verbal observation of your counterpart's emotions, desires, fears, motivations, circumstances, or dynamics.
- It has a specific structure: "It sounds/looks/seems/feels like ..." or "You probably feel/think/want ..."
- Labeling the latent dynamic is more powerful than labeling the presenting dynamic.
- Labels are effective whether they are correct or not.
- It's helpful to Label the positives, but it's *essential* to Label the negatives.

LOW-STAKES PRACTICE

To start getting comfortable with Labels, do these exercises.

1. **Label daily observations.** In casual conversation with strangers or acquaintances (e.g., at the coffee shop, in the elevator, in the checkout line), ask, "How's it going?" Label your counterpart's response and notice how much richer and more detailed their reply is when you use a Label.
2. **Reflect on past conversations.** Think about recent conversations and identify emotions or feelings you could have Labeled. Write them down to build your mental Labeling vocabulary.
3. **Use Labels in customer service interactions.** The next time you're in a conversation with a customer service person, use Labels that acknowledge their situation and emotions. For example, "It seems like this situation happens a lot" or "It sounds like this process is frustrating for customers."

To learn more about Labels, scan the QR code and join the Black Swan Community.

CHAPTER 7

MIRRORS

I am not an avid follower of politics. When it comes to the gory details of who has influence and what's coming down the legislative pipeline, I don't have the first clue. But my wife does—she has to. The government is her biggest client, so it pays for her to rub elbows with political types and keep tabs on their dealings.

That's how I found myself at the Plaza Hotel in Manhattan, in a three-story penthouse that had once belonged to Tommy Hilfiger. My wife had dragged me to some fundraiser cocktail party, and apart from the stunning view of Central Park, there wasn't much for me in that room. Everyone was talking politics—obviously—and I had nothing to say and even less interest in what was being said. I was bored.

So I decided to play a game: Anytime someone talked to me, I would do nothing but Mirror them. As you're about to learn, Mirroring is simply repeating back the last few words your counterpart just said. It's probably the simplest way to keep someone talking without having to say much.

I was sipping my champagne and staring out the window when the owner of the penthouse started talking to me. It was instantly clear that he had no real interest in me; he just wanted to talk. So I started to Mirror him. He told me he had a house in the Hamptons. "The Hamptons?" He told me Sen has the best sushi on the island. "The best sushi?" Every time he paused, I nudged him along with his last few words.

Within fifteen minutes, I had a treasure trove of information about this guy. I knew where his mom lived. I knew what business he was in. I knew who his biggest clients were. I knew who he liked and didn't like in the room. I even knew how much money was in his bank account.

When I told my wife what I had learned, she was stunned. In her experience as a former police officer, people didn't just give away that kind of information. "What did you say to get him to tell you all that?" she asked.

That's the crazy part: nothing. I didn't have to come up with any words of my own. I just gave his own words back to him ... and that's exactly what you're about to learn to do.

WHAT IS A MIRROR?

Mirroring is simply repeating back to your counterpart the last few words they've said, exactly as they said them.

For example:

"We're thinking of moving to a new neighborhood."
"A new neighborhood?"

"I was reviewing our agreement, and I'm confused about the last item."
"The last item."

"I have to give a huge presentation in an hour, and the anticipation is killing me."
"Killing you?"

A Mirror is short: usually one to three words, no more than five. It's a conversational boost—a quick, simple nudge that encourages the other person to keep talking. It replaces tired, generic responses like "tell me more" and "let's unpack that."

Like a Label, a Mirror simultaneously shows you're listening and invites your counterpart to expand on what they've said—thereby revealing more about what they really think, feel, and want. When you give them their words back, they get a dopamine hit; you've helped satisfy that undying urge for someone else to understand them. You've shown that you're interested, which makes you interesting, which makes you eligible for more information.

Note that we're ending some of these Mirrors with a question mark and others with a period. This is meant to indicate the inflection of your voice—up or down—which makes a difference in how your counterpart perceives the Mirror. An upward inflection makes a Mirror sound like a question, whereas a downward inflection acknowledges that you heard them.

Both inflections work; either way, the Mirror will demonstrate that you're listening and encourage the other person to say more. However, as you practice using Mirrors, you'll notice that sometimes an upward inflection feels right—for example, if your counterpart has said something surprising or curious. At other times, an upward inflection feels completely inappropriate.

For example, imagine that someone is telling you about their recent cancer diagnosis and they end with, "I'm just devastated." If you Mirror with an upward inflection ("Devastated?"), it sounds like you're confused about why they're devastated—*not* the impression you want to give. Much better to use a downward inflection ("Devastated."), which sounds like recognition and appreciation.

WHEN TO USE MIRRORS

Mirrors can be used at any point in a conversation. Whenever you want to show particular interest or encourage your counterpart to say more about something, Mirror it. The only caveat here is that you definitely want to avoid interrupting them. If they're on a roll, don't interject with a Mirror. Wait for a pause where it feels appropriate to chime in.

As you get more skilled with Mirrors, you don't have to confine yourself to your counterpart's last few words. If they said something earlier in the sentence (or even several sentences back) that you want to know more about, Mirror it. In that way, you can use Mirrors to guide and redirect the conversation.

For example:

"That kid's behavior is driving me insane—I just don't know what to do about it."
"Driving you insane?"

"I've been meaning to start writing a book, but right now all my time is focused on serving my clients."
"A book?"

"Thailand is my favorite place in the world. We just spent three weeks there, and I can't wait to go back."
"Three weeks!"

The key is that you're repeating their words *verbatim*. That's what gets their attention and shows you're really listening, which is what makes them inclined to keep talking.

THE PITFALLS OF MIRRORING

On paper, Mirroring seems much easier than Labeling. You don't have to worry about using the right structure, digging past the surface, or avoiding the many hazards of Label delivery. All you have to do is repeat a few words your counterpart just said, exactly as they said them.

In reality, people struggle more with Mirrors than with Labels. That speaks volumes about our listening skills—most people are listening so poorly that they can't even repeat what they just heard. This is especially true when you're under pressure, feeling threatened, or otherwise in a negative emotional state.

But if you *are* listening, it's pretty hard to screw up a Mirror. In fact, the most common failure when it comes to Mirroring is the failure to do it at all. You get in your head and think, *This is weird. I'm going to sound like a parrot. They're going to notice I'm doing something strange.* So you don't do it, and you miss the opportunity to build rapport and learn more about the other person.

It's true that if you overdo it, your counterpart will notice. If you throw seven Mirrors in a row at them, of course it will sound unnatural. It will give the impression that you're not really listening. Same if your tone is robotic, stiff, fearful, or otherwise insincere.

Remember, at the heart of it all, you're two human beings in a conversation. Mirroring, just like all the other Black Swan skills, is seasoning for your conversational stew. Don't overdo it. It's better not to use the skills at all than to force them into the conversation every thirty seconds. The harder you think about when and how to use the skill, the less natural it will sound. If you do enough low-stakes practice, your brain will bring up the right skill for you at the right moment.

IN SHORT ...

- Mirroring is simply repeating back to your counterpart the last few words they said, exactly as they said them.
- It's very simple but requires attentive listening.
- Upward inflection makes it a question; downward inflection makes it a confirmation.

LOW-STAKES PRACTICE

To start getting comfortable with Mirrors, do these exercises.

1. **Mirror in work meetings.** During team meetings, use Mirrors to clarify or show engagement:
    - Colleague: "We're struggling to meet deadlines on this project."
    - You: "Struggling to meet deadlines?"

2. **Mirror with customers/clients.** If you work in any customer-facing role, Mirror customer concerns or preferences to build rapport:
    - Client: "We're looking for a more affordable option."
    - You: "A more affordable option?"

3. **Mirror in everyday conversations.** During casual chats with friends or colleagues, repeat the last one to three key words or phrases they say.
    - Friend: "I've been so busy with work."
    - You: "Busy with work?"

To learn more about Mirrors, scan the QR code and join the Black Swan Community.

CHAPTER 8

DYNAMIC SILENCE

In late 2021, the podcaster Lex Fridman interviewed Elon Musk.* At one point in the conversation, Fridman asked Musk when he thought SpaceX would land a human being on Mars. Musk said, "Hmm …" and sat in dead silence for what felt like an eternity, completely still, only his shifting eyes betraying any mental activity. Finally, a full twenty-two seconds after Fridman asked the question, Musk answered, "Best case is about five years, worst case ten years."

This is impressive—not Musk's answer but Fridman's willingness to let that silence sit undisturbed for that long. Most people can't stand that much silence; they would have jumped in after five seconds with some clarification or follow-up question. Especially in a broadcast interview like this, dead air feels painful. But Fridman seemed to know that if he broke that silence, he would also break Musk's train of thought.

---

* Lex Fridman, "Elon Musk: SpaceX, Mars, Tesla Autopilot, Self-Driving, Robotics, and AI | Lex Fridman Podcast #252," YouTube, December 28, 2021, https://www.youtube.com/watch?v=DxREm3s1scA.

He was dead right. Silence is a powerful tool in any conversation, but *especially* in a negotiation. It gives your counterpart space to think and express themselves fully, without feeling pressured to rush. That means they respond with fuller information, more thoughtful decisions, and calmer emotions. In other words, silence gets you closer to the truth.

WHAT IS DYNAMIC SILENCE?

Dynamic Silence is the simple act of NOT talking.

Shutting your mouth.

Deliberately creating a void in the conversation so the other person can think and speak.

For how long? However long it takes for your counterpart to start talking. If you're the one to break the silence, the silence wasn't long enough.

We call it Dynamic Silence for the following reason: To the average person, silence does not appear to accomplish anything, but for Tactical Empathy practitioners, silence is dynamic because it is working even when no one is talking. It influences the other person to contemplate and/or continue talking. And if they are talking, you are learning.

This is even simpler than Mirroring but even harder for most people to do. Most of us feel deeply uncomfortable with silence. We desperately want to fill it. We have all kinds of stories in our heads about why silence is bad: *If I don't say anything, they'll think I have nothing to say. They'll think I'm incompetent or ignorant. They'll think I'm not in control of the conversation.*

Let's go back to the big lesson from chapter 2: *It's not about you.*

When you fill the silence, you make it about you. You don't give them time to think. You make it impossible for the other person to fully digest and think through what you're telling them. Even worse, you make it impossible for them to say what they think, feel, and want. Then how are you supposed to get to the truth? You can't. You're stuck in your own head.

But the beauty of silence is that as much as you want to fill it, *they* want to fill it too. Most people are just as uncomfortable with silence as you are. It's a question of who is willing to wait it out longer. If you want information, you better be the one who waits.

So forget the stories in your head. What *really* happens when you give your counterpart silence is they see a clear demonstration of your intent to maintain two-way dialogue. This nonthreatening communication skill causes them to think more clearly and give you more information—which is precisely what you want in any negotiation.

WHEN TO USE DYNAMIC SILENCE

We introduce Dynamic Silence here because it's crucial to the success of your Labels and Mirrors. If you don't follow a Label or Mirror with Dynamic Silence, it *will not work*. Not implementing Dynamic Silence is like driving through a stop sign into a busy intersection. You *must* give your counterpart time to digest what you've said and respond. Do not derail their train of thought. Do not cut off their opportunity to express themselves. *Wait* for them to speak.

It might take two seconds of silence for that to happen. It might take ten. It might take a whole minute. It depends on the context and your counterpart's personality. Each of the three different Negotiator Personality Types (as you'll see in chapter 15) has a different feeling about silence. Analysts in particular *love* silence and want to use it as time to think. They will tolerate much longer silences, and if you interrupt their thinking, you turn yourself back into a threat for them.

So whenever you drop a Label or a Mirror, shut your mouth and keep it zipped. The same goes for any time you deliver important information or pose a question. Resist the urge to expand on what you've just said.

Let it land. Give it room to breathe. Don't step on it. Wait patiently for your counterpart to respond.

This is especially important if you think they're not going to like what you've just said. When you turn someone down, when you make a request, when you reveal your price, when you ask them to make a tough decision—these are the moments when you will feel most tempted to run your mouth because you're afraid to find out what your counterpart will say. But your extra words only work against you; they undermine your point and invade your counterpart's space to think and express themselves. Just be quiet and wait.

You can also use Dynamic Silence to great effect after your *counterpart* says something. Don't respond right away. Give yourself time to think. Chances are high that in that moment of silence, they will get so uncomfortable that they'll say more—give you more information, explain more of their thoughts and feelings, maybe even reveal a black swan. All because you gave them silence. You gave them space, and they felt compelled to fill it.

This is especially effective when they've just lashed out at you. Most people find it hard to fight with someone who doesn't fight back. When they attack, they expect a defense or retaliation. If you give them nothing—just Dynamic Silence—the force of the attack often dissipates quickly. Instead of continuing to attack, they're likely to calm down and possibly explain their motivations, soften their words, or even apologize.

Silence helps dissipate your negative emotions in that moment as well. It gives you a moment to internally Label how you feel (disrespected, ashamed, betrayed—whatever it is), and as you've learned, the act of Labeling a negative emotion reduces its intensity. This helps you avoid saying something in the heat of the moment that you'll later regret.

The only time to break a silence is if you say something that visibly upsets the other person. Don't let them stew in their negative emotions. Break the silence to Label that affect shift with something like, "It looks like I said something that doesn't sit well with you." Then shut your mouth and wait.

PITFALLS OF DYNAMIC SILENCE

There's really just one obstacle here: It's hard to stay silent, especially when you're just starting to practice these skills. Our advice? Use a mantra to hold back the urge to speak. Personally, I like to repeat "Dynamic Silence … Dynamic Silence … Dynamic Silence …" in my head over and over. Some people like to count. Chris's son Brandon likes to pinch the web between his thumb and index finger. Try those, or make up some other mental or physical reminder to keep quiet.

As uncomfortable as you are, your counterpart is just as uncomfortable. They will want to break the silence to get comfortable again. You just have to be more disciplined than they are; it's a trained skill, and the more you practice, the easier it gets.

Everybody always asks, How long do I have to wait? *As long as it takes*. There is no rule—it depends on the situation. Read your counterpart's reaction. Gather data with your eyes. If they look upset, don't wait. If it looks like they're still processing, wait and keep waiting until they speak up. It's that simple.

IN SHORT …

- Dynamic Silence is the simple act of *not* talking.
- You *must* use Dynamic Silence after every Label and every Mirror.
- Do *not* be the one to break the silence. Give your counterpart the space to digest what you've said and respond.

LOW-STAKES PRACTICE

To start getting comfortable with Dynamic Silence, do these exercises.

1. **After Labeling or asking a question, zip it.** These are the moments when your counterpart needs time to think and express themselves. Don't interrupt that process. Watch, listen, and reflect on what you're observing in your counterpart.
2. **Pause before answering a question.** Don't rush to answer immediately. Give yourself time to think. Take at least two deep breaths—or more, if you want—before speaking.
3. **Use silence to prompt your counterpart.** When speaking one-on-one with someone, refrain from responding as soon as they finish a thought. Instead, stay silent and maintain eye contact to encourage them to expand on that thought.

To learn more about Dynamic Silence, scan the QR code and join the Black Swan Community.

CHAPTER 9

SUMMARY

Imagine you're meeting a friend for lunch, and she walks in looking harried and beleaguered—definitely not her usual bubbly self. Before you even ask, she launches into the story of her week from hell.

"Last weekend," she tells you, "I was on my way home from the grocery store, almost to the house, when my neighbor's stupid sixteen-year-old son backed his car right into me. Of course, his car barely has a dent, but he smashed up my front wheel and headlights. The damage isn't that bad, but the car isn't drivable.

"My neighbor was so embarrassed, and he's a good guy—I've known him for a few years now. He said he wanted to take care of things under the table so his son wouldn't have an accident on his record, and I was like, OK, fine. I trust you, I know where you live—it's not like you're going to disappear on me.

"But now it's been a week, and I haven't heard a peep from him. I've had to use ride-sharing all week long, and with the kids and everything, it's *such* a hassle. I have to get a ride to work, then another one to pick up the kids at school, and another to take them to practice, and another one to the store … I'm sick of it. Plus, it's so expensive, and I don't even know if this guy is gonna pay me back for all that. He's not even returning my calls.

"I was trying to be a good neighbor and do him a favor, and this is what I get. I guess no good deed goes unpunished. I'm at my wit's end."

What do you say to make her feel understood? You already have a couple of tools in your toolbox for this: Labels and Mirrors. However, after an information dump like this, one Label or Mirror doesn't quite feel like enough. You need something more substantial to show that you really caught everything your friend was throwing at you.

Enter the Summary.

WHAT IS A SUMMARY?

> *A Summary is a detailed rundown of everything your counterpart has shared so far about their situation and how they feel about it—the facts, the events, the circumstances, the emotions, and the dynamics.*

It's the world according to your counterpart, in *your* words.

The structure of a Summary is simple. Start with "So far you've told me …" or "What we've discussed so far is …" and follow it with a replay in your own words of the information they've shared and the feelings they've expressed, explicitly or implicitly. Unlike a Label, this is not a short, one-sentence affair; if you were to write a Summary down, it would be at least nine bullet points.

For example, imagine your spouse has spent the last ten minutes ranting about how you're not doing your fair share of the housework. A Summary might sound like:

So far you've told me …

- You feel I'm not doing my fair share of the work at home.
- You're busier than ever at work, and you're exhausted at the end of the day.
- You come home to find dirty laundry, dirty dishes, and a mess in every room.
- You feel like you're always the one who has to drive the kids and do the grocery shopping, too.
- You recognize that I also have a demanding job.
- It's frustrating for you to see me relaxing when there are still chores to do.
- When you start cleaning up and I don't offer to help, you feel taken for granted.
- You think I'm setting a bad example for the kids, who also never offer to help.
- You're tired of always having to ask after all these years.
- You sometimes want to just disappear and see how we survive without you.
- You worry that these seemingly trivial issues will pile up and tear us apart.

When you've covered everything, follow your Summary with Dynamic Silence. Wait patiently and observe what your counterpart gives back to you. Ideally, it's emotional buy-in—some indication that you've hit the nail on the head and made them feel understood. They might give you more information to fill in a gap or correct something you didn't get quite right.

Notice that this example Summary includes *a lot* of information. It should; ten minutes of ranting covers a lot of ground. The Summary needs to capture *all* of it, or as much as you can possibly recall.

We can't emphasize enough: What makes a Summary so powerful is that it's *comprehensive*. It pulls together all the important information your counterpart has shared with you so far. To notice, remember, and reflect back that much information, you have to *really* listen. You have to get out of your own head, set aside your own goals and concerns, and truly make the conversation about the other person.

Reflecting all that information back shows your counterpart just how closely you're listening. It fulfills their deep, instinctive desire to be heard and understood. Many of the tools in the Tactical Empathy toolbox do that, but a Summary is one of the most robust and powerful for this purpose. A Label or Mirror shows that you heard what they *just* said a moment ago. A Summary shows that you heard the full story—not just that you got the overall gist but that you noticed all the important details.

That's extremely compelling. As we've said before, most people never get listened to on that level, not even by their loved ones. So when you demonstrate that you've been paying that kind of attention, it's a revelation. They get a huge hit of those feel-good hormones that make them relax, let down their guard, and open up to you. You've made them feel valued and respected, and they will instinctively want to return the favor.

WHEN TO USE A SUMMARY

A Summary can be used anytime, but there are five places in a conversation where you *must* use it. By that we mean that these are the moments when a Summary will do you the most good—and the failure to use one could set you back significantly.

1. At the beginning of the conversation

In most sensitive conversations, the situation at hand began well before the current conversation. In other words, there is a backstory. You already have some information about your counterpart's situation and their feelings about it. A Summary is the perfect way to open the conversation by making it about them. It shows that you're attuned to their perspective, not your own goals. Right from the start, you're removing yourself as a threat in the conversation.

When you use a Summary to open a conversation (and only in that case), it's a good idea to follow it with a question: "What did I miss?" This turns the conversation over to the other person in a deferential way. You're extending the olive branch, showing that you're as concerned with their worldview as your own. It's an unusual move to make, and that little surprise often makes people drop their guard. That said, we want to reiterate that you should *only* ask this question when you're using the Summary to open a conversation—not at any other time.

To see why a Summary is such a good conversation opener, consider the alternatives. For most people, the default is to start a sensitive conversation by stating their own objectives. Whether they do so in a direct, blunt way or a more subtle, gentle way doesn't really matter—they're making the conversation about them, not their counterpart. Another common way to start is with a question, which isn't quite as bad, but it can still raise your counterpart's defenses; a question puts all the pressure on them to explain themselves to someone who—as far as they know—doesn't understand anything about their situation.

See? Much better to start with a Summary of whatever information you've gleaned so far about the other person's perspective. It puts everyone on the same page about why you're there and what the purpose of the conversation is, while at the same time helping to remove you as a threat to your counterpart.

2. Prior to being assertive

Let's go back for a second to the definition of Tactical Empathy: It's the art of influencing others by articulating what they're thinking and feeling, *without* necessarily agreeing, disagreeing, or sympathizing. You *can* disagree with your counterpart. At some point, you *will* disagree with your counterpart. And because your goal in the conversation is to get to the truth, the last thing you want to do is hide that disagreement from them or pretend it doesn't exist.

However, you *do* need to express your disagreement in a way that doesn't make them feel attacked, and the Summary is precisely the tool for doing that. Before you express your thoughts and feelings, give your counterpart a thorough, robust Summary of their thoughts and feelings. You don't have to condone them; you just have to *say* them. That verbal recognition makes them feel like you respect their perspective and their right to hold it. Only then are they ready to hear how your perspective differs without putting their walls up and shutting you out.

(In this situation, where you're going to tell them something or make an ask they might not like, there's another powerful tool that should follow your Summary. It's called an Accusations Audit, and you'll learn all about it in the next chapter.)

3. Anytime you need clarification

As you're listening to your counterpart, you might notice gaps in your understanding. They might say something that doesn't make sense to you, gloss over something that seems important, express two things that seem contradictory, or never actually get to a clear point. A Summary is an excellent way to clear up any confusion.

As always, start with "So far, you've said …" and repeat back (in your own words) all the key points you can recall.

4. Anytime you're going to make an offer or counteroffer

In this situation, a Summary serves to open your counterpart's mind to your offer before you put it on the table. By using it before making an offer (or counter), you're demonstrating that you have a keen grasp of the entirety of the environment, the stakes, and their perspective before presenting your offer. That makes them far more likely to seriously consider the offer and view it in a positive light, even if it's not exactly what they want.

5. To ensure implementation of your agreement

Using a Summary at the end of the conversation helps dramatically increase the likelihood that whatever you've agreed to will actually happen. As we'll discuss in more detail in chapter 17, a yes without a how is worthless. So before you walk away from your counterpart, Summarize exactly what you've agreed to and all the details of how it will be implemented.

Watch how they respond. If it's not with enthusiastic buy-in, that's a sign your agreement isn't as final as you think it is, and they might not follow through on it. If you observe that dynamic, don't let it go. Instead, Label it. Bring it out into the open and see if you can unearth the hesitations, doubts, or obstacles that haven't been addressed yet. If you close the conversation without using a Summary and getting strong buy-in, you run a very high risk of having your "agreement" fall apart after you walk away.

PITFALLS OF SUMMARIES

Summaries are pretty simple and straightforward. There are just a few common ways to screw them up, so let's address those now.

1. Making it about you

The entire purpose of a Summary is to thoroughly articulate your understanding of the environment as well as your counterpart's thoughts and feelings. It's not about what *you* think at all. For that reason, the opening line should not have an "I" anywhere near it.

"So far, you said …"

"What we've discussed so far is …"

Not "What I heard you say is …"

This may seem like silly semantics, but words matter—that's the whole idea behind this book. While you probably won't blow up the whole conversation by starting with "I," it's better to keep the focus off yourself as much as possible.

This is true throughout the rest of the Summary as well. Avoid using any "I" statements, like "I noticed/saw/heard/think/guess …" Stick to "you" or "we" statements whenever possible.

2. Not saying enough

This is a very common problem we see with Summaries. We said earlier that you should aim to cover at least nine points. That's not some magic number backed by research; we just started asking for that because at our training events, people's Summaries never went deep enough. Nine is a lot, and aiming for it forces you to pay closer attention to the conversation and give a more robust reflection of your counterpart's perspective.

We can't emphasize this enough: A short, shallow Summary will not work well. Just imagine you and I have been talking for thirty minutes, and I want to tell you why I disagree with you. If I just give you a couple sentences that capture the gist of your perspective, then launch into *my* point of view, how are you going to feel? Like I was just listening to respond. Like I don't understand half the story and don't really care to try. Immediately, your defenses are back up and your mind is closed to what I'm saying.

Depth and rigor are what make a Summary effective—that's what shows how deeply you're listening. Again, you don't have to agree with what your counterpart is saying. You just acknowledge it by saying it back to them.

3. Not doing it at all

The greatest mistake people make with Summaries is not using them at all. Unlike the other skills you've learned so far, a Summary isn't a quick thing you can throw out in a couple of seconds. It feels like a lot of work, and it puts the brakes on the conversation. Most people are in such a rush to get to their objective that they would rather charge ahead than slow down and use a Summary.

But we told you at the very beginning of this book: Tactical Empathy slows you down to speed you up. Yes, a Summary puts the brakes on the conversation. It slows you down *on purpose* because you *need* to slow down to make sure your counterpart feels understood. But once that happens—once they take down their defenses and open up to truly collaborating with you—the rest of the process is much faster and easier.

You get to charge forward with an enthusiastic ally instead of dragging a reluctant partner or battling an outright enemy.

CASE STUDY RESOLUTION

At our live training events, we often use stories—like the one at the beginning of this chapter about the car accident—to practice Summaries. Invariably, the first responses hardly qualify as Summaries at all. It's usually something like, "What you've said so far is that you got in a car accident last week, and you're angry that you still don't have your car back."

That's a little better than the typical (non–Tactical Empathy) response, which is something along the lines of "Wow, that sucks." While not inaccurate, it doesn't even begin to capture the important details about what happened and how the storyteller is feeling. If it were you, how would that attempt at a Summary make you feel? Probably like your friend wasn't really paying attention and doesn't want to hear you whine about your crappy week.

Capturing all the key details—the facts of what happened as well as the thoughts and emotions around those events—is critical to delivering a quality Summary. Here's what that might sound like in this situation:

So far you've told me that ...

- Your neighbor's kid, who clearly wasn't paying attention, backed into your car.
- It barely damaged his own car but put yours out of commission.
- You feel frustrated because things like these are never easy ...
- And your neighbor is complicating it more by ghosting you.
- You're dealing with a certain level of anger and betrayal because you trusted him at his word that he would take care of the damage, under the table.

- It sounds like you are also wondering how he duped you into thinking he was a good guy.
- Now, a week later, you're still ride-sharing for every trip …
- Which is difficult, with having to get a ride to work, then another one to pick up the kids at school, and another to take them to practice, and another to get to the store …
- And you're sick and tired of it.
- Plus, it's expensive and you are worried about that in addition to what the repairs will cost if he doesn't pay for the damage.
- It feels like you are struggling with what to do next.

Yes, it's long—and that's exactly why it works. When your friend hears this, she'll breathe a huge sigh of relief. *Finally*, someone understands what she's going through. And with her emotions calmed, she might actually be open to your input on how to resolve the situation.

BONUS SKILL: PARAPHRASING

Now that you've learned about both Labels and Summaries, we can introduce you to the in-between skill: Paraphrasing. A Label is short and sweet, usually less than ten words. A Summary is long and comprehensive, covering at least nine pieces of information. Paraphrasing occupies the space in between.

It's exactly what it sounds like. You're simply rephrasing what they've said in your own words, usually in one to three sentences. Paraphrasing serves the same two purposes as the other skills: It shows your counterpart that you're listening and encourages them to share more information.

We mention this skill almost in passing because it's not something that requires a lot of explanation and practice. If you focus on mastering Labels and Summaries, Paraphrasing will happen naturally. On the flip side, if you focus on trying to Paraphrase, you're likely to end up with either a run-on Label or a weak Summary.

So don't worry about mastering this skill. Labels and Summaries are much more important and much more counterintuitive. It will take awareness and persistence to master them, and when you do, they will make a huge difference in every sensitive conversation you have.

IN SHORT ...

- A Summary is a detailed rundown of everything your counterpart has shared about their situation and how they feel about it—the facts, the events, the circumstances, the emotions, and the dynamics.
- It starts with "So far you've told me ..." or "What we've discussed so far is ..."
- To work, a Summary needs to be robust. Aim to include at least nine pieces of information that your counterpart has given you.
- Use a Summary at the beginning of the conversation, prior to being assertive, when you need clarification, when you're going to make an offer or counteroffer, and to ensure implementation of your agreement.
- The most common mistake is not using Summaries at all. They will slow the conversation down, but that is a good thing. Taking the time to make your counterpart feel understood now will save you more time later.

LOW-STAKES PRACTICE

To start getting comfortable with Summaries, do these exercises:

1. **Practice with podcasts.** After listening to a short podcast or an interview, summarize the main points to yourself or someone else. Try to hit at least nine pieces of information.
2. **Use Summaries with customer service.** When speaking with customer service representatives, Summarize what they've told you to confirm your understanding.
3. **Use Summaries in work meetings.** During team meetings, Summarize a colleague's point before responding or adding your input.
4. **Use Summaries in family discussions.** In a family conversation, Summarize someone's opinion or feelings to validate that you understand their perspective.

To learn more about Summaries, scan the QR code and join the Black Swan Community.

PART III

THE BEST OF THE REST

The Core Four will be your bread and butter in any sensitive conversation, but there's plenty more in the Black Swan toolbox. The following chapters cover the most important of those tools, the ones we find ourselves using time and time again. Here's what you're about to learn:

- How to deliver a message your counterpart doesn't want to hear
- How to use your tone of voice to influence their emotions
- How to ask questions that shape their thinking
- How to gently keep the conversation moving
- How to confront persistent counterproductive behavior

CHAPTER 10

ACCUSATIONS AUDIT

Several years ago, a woman—let's call her Jade—reached out to The Black Swan Group for negotiation coaching at the eleventh hour. Everything about the deal had already been screwed up, and she was looking for a lifeline.

The backstory was that a couple of years earlier, she had arranged a family retreat at a very expensive, exclusive resort. During that trip, her father, who suffered from nerve damage in his lower extremities, somehow ended up soaking in a hot tub that was way too hot. He landed in the emergency room with severe burns from the waist down.

The resort's insurance company realized they were probably going to have to eat this, so they offered to pay damages. Their initial offer was $1,000, but Jade's family didn't respond. Then they offered $5,000. No response. They upped it to $10,000. Still no response.

As it turned out, Jade's mother had said she was taking care of the issue, but in fact she was just ignoring the insurance company's letters. By the time Jade realized this, the statute of limitations on the case was going to run out in a month. Of course, the insurance company knew this, too. All they had to do was drag their feet for a few more weeks, and they would be free of any obligation to compensate Jade's father at all.

Jade was, understandably, horrified. She was angry, aggressive, and caught up in her own emotions about the agony her father had suffered and the negligence her mother had displayed. When it came to negotiating with the insurance company, her instinct was to go in with guns blazing. She wanted to give them a taste of her family's pain.

If you've been paying attention so far, red flags should be waving madly in your mind. She was feeling highly threatened—all her defenses were up, she wasn't thinking clearly, and she certainly wasn't ready to collaborate with her counterpart. She was making it all about her, not them. If she went into the conversation like that, pointing fingers and demanding justice, her counterpart would feel threatened too. That's a great way to get to an impasse—and in this case, an impasse would be a big loss for Jade.

This is an extreme example of something we all experience pretty frequently: having to ask someone for something. We do it every day, in big and small ways. We ask the kids to get out the door on time in the morning; we ask the barista for a double-shot, half-caff, no-foam oat milk latte; we ask a client to renew a million-dollar contract. In those situations, we're usually so wrapped up in what we want that we completely fail to address the other person's perspective. As a result, their first response to our ask is resistance, even if the request is a small one.

Enter the Accusations Audit. This technique flips our instinct on its head. It forces us to get out of our own minds and make the other person feel understood *before* we make any ask—which goes a long way toward getting the response we want, and getting it willingly instead of reluctantly.

The Accusations Audit isn't just for making asks; it's for any situation where your counterpart might respond with resistance. Breaking bad news, giving tough feedback, telling them something they might not want to hear—these are all perfect opportunities to use an Accusations Audit. This is one of the most useful and versatile tools in your Tactical Empathy toolbox, and you're about to see why.

WHAT IS AN ACCUSATIONS AUDIT?

An Accusations Audit is an inventory and audit of the possible negative things the other side might be thinking about you or the conversation based on the circumstances, environment, or their own paranoia.

It's a series of preemptive Labels that proactively address every bad thing they might be thinking or feeling about you, the circumstances, or the conversation, based on reality or their imagination.

An Accusations Audit has a very specific structure, starting with: "You're probably thinking/feeling …" Or, if you know for sure, "I know you think/feel …"

For example:

- "You probably think I'm the worst partner in the world."
- "You're going to want to fire me."
- "You must feel like everyone is laughing at you behind your back."
- And Derek's personal favorite: "You're going to want to reach through the screen and stab me in the eye with a pen."

Notice that we said an Accusations Audit should cover every bad thing they *might* be thinking or feeling. That includes negative things they haven't expressed at all yet, not even with their body language. You're really going out on a limb with your hypotheses here.

This achieves two things. One is that it shows you're coming from a position where it's not about you—it's about them. The other is that it gives them the opportunity to brace themselves for what you're about to say next, which they may not like. Just like in a car crash or a fistfight, bracing for impact helps mitigate the pain and damage.

This is the most counterintuitive of all the skills. You're taking a negative light and pointing it back on yourself, which feels extremely risky. People *hate* to do this because they're terrified it will make the other person think and feel all the negative things contained in the Accusations Audit. Some believe it is tantamount to a confession or admission of guilt.

But as you learned in chapter 4 and again in chapter 6, it's impossible to plant a negative. If they weren't thinking or feeling the negative thing, they won't start just thinking or feeling it because you said it—they'll correct you. If they *were* thinking or feeling the negative thing, it's a good thing you said it, because it shows that you understand their perspective. That immediately takes the edge off the negativity and clears the way for a more productive conversation.

HOW TO PREPARE AN ACCUSATIONS AUDIT

The first step is to go back to the CAVIAAR process you learned in chapter 2.

- **Curiosity:** Choose to be curious about what's driving your counterpart.
- **Acceptance:** Accept in advance that you will be attacked.
- **Venting:** Speak all your own negative thoughts and emotions out loud to clear them so you're less likely to get defensive and reactive.
- **Identifying:** Try to pinpoint what kind of person your counterpart is (more on that in chapter 15) and how they're approaching the situation.

- *Accusations Audit:* Now you can prepare what you want to say with a clear mind and calm emotions.
- **Remembering:** Remind yourself that the other person is not your enemy—the ultimate goal is to collaborate and come to an agreement.

Notice that before you're ready to even think about the Accusations Audit, you need to put yourself in the right headspace. As we just said, shining a negative light on yourself is totally counterintuitive and supremely uncomfortable. Getting defensive will only get in the way of preparing an effective Accusations Audit. So before you get started, take the time to go through CAVI (the first four steps of the CAVIAAR process) and get into an open, calm, and curious state of mind.

Once you've done that, your next step is to brainstorm a comprehensive list of all the negative thoughts, feelings, assumptions, impressions, and dynamics your counterpart could possibly be experiencing. Think about the conversation you need to have with them—whether it's about addressing a conflict, closing a deal, breaking bad news, or something else—and put yourself on their side of the street. Imagine being in their position, given everything you know about them. Then ask yourself:

- If I were them, what would I be thinking about me?
- What are the absolute worst interpretations they could have of this situation?
- What are the absolute worst assumptions they could be making about me, my intentions, and my motivations?
- What would be the worst-nightmare outcome for them in this situation?
- How would they feel if that worst-nightmare outcome came true? How would they react?
- What is at stake for them? What are they afraid of losing?

- Who are they going to blame if this situation goes sideways?
- If they were at home with friends and a few drinks, what trash would they be talking about me and this whole situation?

(Note: AI can be a great thought partner in this process. To learn more about how we used AI to brainstorm for Accusations Audits, see the appendix.)

The rule of thumb here is *overkill*. More is more. The more Accusations Audits you come up with, the better. The more visceral they sound, the better—and by visceral, we mean that your words should pack a punch. Don't beat around the bush or try to soften the harshness; instead, do the opposite. Your goal is to overshoot their actual negative thoughts and feelings by a mile—better yet, by a thousand miles. Turn off your inner editor and just write down everything you can possibly think of in the harshest terms, even if it sounds stupid or outrageous.

- "You probably think I'm playing fast and loose with the money." ➔
  "I know you think I'm a lying, cheating thief."
- "You're probably going to be mad at me." ➔
  "You're going to want to strangle me with a lamp cord."

Going extreme feels scary, but it actually works in your favor in two ways. One is that it surprises your counterpart. Most people would never say such harsh things about themselves or be so brutally honest. They're thinking you're either crazy or fearless. In any case, you've just said all the negative things they were going to use as weapons against you, so those things aren't weapons anymore. Your counterpart is thrown off kilter and no longer poised to attack. On the contrary, they're probably thinking you're some kind of mind reader because you're saying things they've thought to themselves but haven't expressed yet.

The second way this tactic works for you is by anchoring them on something much worse than reality. The goal of your super-visceral Accusations Audits is to get your counterpart to conjure up the worst possible things in their mind—their worst fears about the situation. That way, when you deliver the actual ask or news, it seems benign in comparison. You had them going so far into their nightmare scenario that the reality feels like a relief, even though it's probably not what they wanted.

Once you've come up with a thorough list of Accusations Audits, put that list in order from the *most to least* harsh. Resist the urge to trim your list; whatever you leave off is sure to be exactly the thing they skewer you with when the time comes.

When you deliver your Accusations Audits, you'll start at number two on the list and go down, saving number one—the most visceral of them all—for last. This comes from Law of Negotiation Gravity #7: The last impression is the lasting impression. You want to end on your strongest note, not your weakest.

HOW TO DELIVER AN ACCUSATIONS AUDIT

First and most importantly, an Accusations Audit is *best* delivered face-to-face, or at least voice-to-voice. Can it be effective via email or text? Yes … to a degree. But ideally, text or email should be used to drive your counterpart to a voice-to-voice interaction. It's crucial for them to hear your tone, and it's equally crucial for you to observe their response in real time. So, if you have not already arranged to talk, the first step is to request a meeting to have this conversation.

Before you enter that meeting, it's a good idea to revisit the V in CAVIAAR: Venting. We often call this "emptying your bucket." Imagine you're walking around carrying a bucket of your own negativity—your stress, anxiety, anger, frustration, guilt, and other mental baggage. If that bucket is full to the brim, the slightest little bump from anyone else is going to make you spill. That's the last thing you want in a sensitive conversation where your goal is to defuse the *other* person's negativity. Bringing your own crap into the mix makes it impossible to keep the conversation focused on them.

So, empty your bucket. Label your own negative thoughts and feelings *out loud*, including the ones that have nothing to do with the conversation you're about to have. Take deep breaths and let those feelings move through you and out. The emptier your bucket is when you walk into that meeting, the better your chances are of staying calm and focused on them, even if they lash out at you.

Once you enter the conversation, begin by bracing them for what's coming: "You're not going to like what I'm about to say."

Dynamic Silence.

Then, in a low, slow tone of voice, start delivering your Accusations Audits.

Accusations Audit #2 (remember, you're saving #1 for last).

Dynamic Silence for at least one slow, deep breath.

Accusations Audit #3.

Dynamic Silence.

Accusations Audit #4.

Dynamic Silence.

Accusations Audit #5.

Dynamic Silence.

Watch your counterpart's body language closely as you do this. They might shake their head, indicating you're way off base and they want to correct you. They might nod, indicating you've hit on a negative thought or feeling they're actually having that needs to be addressed. They might frown, smile, grimace, or roll their eyes.

All these things are indicators that they have something to express, so be sure to give them *plenty* of Dynamic Silence. Err on the side of too much. Whatever they're thinking might be difficult for them to say, and they need time to put it into words or work up the nerve to say those words out loud. Cut off the silence too soon, and you make yourself into a threat again, which is the opposite of what you want.

Remember the rules of delivering Labels? Likewise, when delivering Accusations Audits, *never* follow them with "but," "and," or "because." You will feel a need to explain what you just said. *Don't.* Don't defend yourself. Don't deny the negative thing you just verbalized. Whenever you feel those words on the tip of your tongue, replace them with Dynamic Silence. You'll get a chance to explain why all those Accusations Audits are not true, but not yet. The time for explanation is later in the conversation. Wait for it.

Here's the hardest part: You have to *keep going* with the Accusations Audit until your counterpart gives you the signal to stop. That signal may sound like:

- "I wasn't thinking those things."
- "You're being too hard on yourself."
- "Now you're scaring me."
- "It can't be that bad."
- "Can we just rip the Band-Aid off?"

They might say nothing but show you with their body language that enough is enough—for example, by holding up a hand to cut you off.

We can't stress this enough: If you proceed before you have permission, you are focused on yourself, not them. Do not move on from your list of Accusations Audits until the other person signals that they're ready for you to proceed. Only when you've received a clear signal is it safe to deliver the bad news or make the ask.

Remember that you should save Accusations Audit #1—the harshest, most cutting one—for last. If they stop you before you get to it, apologize for wasting their time and then deliver the #1 Audit, beginning with "I know you …"

If you get through all your Accusations and they still don't respond, let the Dynamic Silence sit longer—at least 10 seconds. If they still say nothing, use a Label that invites them to correct you: "It seems like I'm way off the mark" or "It seems like I've missed something."

We can't overemphasize that the harsher you go, the better. People appreciate being given a chance to brace themselves. When you do that properly, they will accept almost anything.

WHEN TO USE AN ACCUSATIONS AUDIT

There's no bad time to use an Accusations Audit, but they are *mandatory* in three places.

1. At the beginning of the conversation

Before you get to the nuts and bolts of a sensitive conversation, it's crucial to clear the negatives out of the other person's head. This is true even if the lead-up to the meeting has been amicable. They know you want something from them, which automatically makes you a threat on some level.

Accusations Audits are the fastest way to remove yourself as a threat and build trust. Open the conversation with a Summary (from chapter 9) to set the stage. Then, follow the Summary with an Accusations Audit that defuses their negative emotions around whatever you're about to tell them or ask them.

If you skip this step, they can't listen to you because those negatives are still bouncing around in their mind, distracting them from your message. Their hackles are still raised; they're on the defense, consciously or subconsciously, so they're not open to new information. They also can't think clearly, so they're not as smart as they otherwise would be.

To put a visual image to all this, imagine their head as a hopper full of ping-pong balls—negative thoughts and emotions about this interaction. You need to remove as many as possible, and the only way to do that is to call them out explicitly.

2. Before delivering bad news

An Accusations Audit is essential anytime you're going to tell the other person something they don't want to hear. Maybe you have to say no to a request. Maybe you have to give them a counteroffer they're not going to love. Maybe you have to bring their unreasonable expectations down to earth. Maybe you have to give them tough feedback or say something that might hurt their feelings.

If there's even a small chance they might not be thrilled with what you're about to say, preface it with an Accusations Audit.

3. Before an ask

Anytime you want someone to do something for you (accept your proposal, complete a task, etc.), start with an Accusations Audit. If your ask is innocuous (something you know they'll agree to), you can do a scaled-down version of an Accusations Audit, with just one or two Labels followed by Dynamic Silence. Even though you know they'll say yes, the Accusations Audit makes it go down easier because you have demonstrated an understanding of their perspective and circumstances. You create a willing partner instead of a reluctant one, which is crucial because (as you know) revenge is a powerful motivator. A reluctant partner may agree now, but they'll make life hard for you however they can in the future. An Accusations Audit will help you avoid that.

4. To deweaponize "fairness"

In a typical negotiation, it's not uncommon to hear something like this right at the beginning of the conversation: "I'm only here for a fair deal" or "I want to be fair to you and you to be fair to me" or "I just want what's fair."

This is what Derek calls *weaponizing fairness*. It's putting you on notice that if you disagree with anything they say, they're going to call it unfair. It makes you uncomfortable, and as human beings, when we're uncomfortable, we'll do just about anything to get comfortable again. In this situation, that might mean doing things that are against our best interests just to avoid being accused of unfairness.

To nip this in the bud, Derek coaches all his clients to use the following Accusations Audit at the beginning of any negotiation: "If at any point during this conversation you think I'm being unfair, I want you to stop me, and we'll rewind the conversation to where the unfairness began and go from there." (Derek likes to illustrate that "rewind" with his hands—try it when you use this line.)

You probably noticed that this doesn't follow the typical Accusations Audit structure. However, in practice, it still acts like a preemptive Label. In Derek's opinion, this is the one Accusations Audit you can't do without, because it lays the groundwork for a productive, honest conversation.

CASE STUDY RESOLUTION

Now that you understand what an Accusations Audit is and how to use it, let's go back to Jade and the insurance company. Left to her own devices, Jade would have gone into that conversation making it all about her—her feelings, her assumptions, her demands. She was enraged and looking to collect her pound of flesh.

It took a long time to convince her to start with the Accusations Audit before she asked for anything. But she finally agreed to sit down with us and think about all the negative thoughts and feelings the insurance representative might be harboring about her, the circumstances, or the conversation they needed to have. Here's some of what we came up with, in no particular order:

- "You probably think we're an entitled family just trying to impose our will."
- "You probably think we're so rich that we don't need the money."
- "You probably feel like we're just being greedy."

- "You're probably wondering why it took us three years to respond to you."
- "You're probably frustrated with my family's poor communication."
- "You probably feel like this puts an undue burden on you."
- "You probably think I'm trying to complicate your life by pushing you to come up with some kind of recourse at the last minute."

We told Jade to lead with this if she got the opportunity for a real-time conversation with the insurance rep. As it turned out, she did. She hadn't even gotten through half of her Accusations Audit before the rep said, "Stop—I appreciate what you're saying. What can we do to make this better for everyone?"

By the end of the conversation, Jade was able to get a $25,000 settlement without ever having to explain, pitch, or ask for anything ... and that only happened because she went in thinking about the other side's perspective instead of her own.

MORE REAL-WORLD EXAMPLES
Resolving a High-Stakes Mother-Daughter Conflict

Lisa had just gone through a very difficult divorce, which resulted in her two teenage sons choosing to live with their father full time. Her twelve-year-old daughter, Riley, was teetering on the edge of making the same choice, and Lisa was desperate to prevent that from happening. However, she still needed to be an effective parent.

One week, she noticed that Riley had been up late on her phone for several days in a row. She was waking up moody and argumentative. So the next night, Lisa took Riley's phone out of the bedroom and put it in the kitchen. This provoked a screaming rant: "It's *my* phone! Dad got it for me, and I'm entitled to use it whenever I want! You have all these stupid rules! You're so mean to me! I can't do anything here! I want to go live with Dad!"

That scared Lisa. She didn't know how to move the conversation forward without pushing her daughter away. That's when she came to us for guidance, and we helped her create an Accusations Audit:

- "You probably think I'm too caught up in my own problems to care about yours."
- "It might seem like I'm choosing my personal interests over spending quality time with you."
- "You might feel like I don't understand what you're going through right now."
- "You could be feeling like I'm not making enough effort to be a part of your life."
- "It seems like you might believe moving in with your dad is the only way to feel heard."
- "You may think I don't value our time together."
- "It might look like I'm not trying hard enough to mend our relationship."
- "You could be worried I'll always put my needs before yours."
- "It might feel like I don't see how much you're hurting."
- "You probably wonder if things will ever get better between us."

Opening with Accusations Audits brought Riley into the conversation and helped her articulate what she really wanted: to have more independence and make more decisions for herself. This blowup wasn't really about the phone or living with her dad. It was about not having certain needs met and not being able to communicate about them.

Talking about these desires openly helped Riley see that threatening to leave didn't actually help her get what she wanted. It also allowed Lisa to come up with some ways Riley could exercise independence in a constructive way, without making unhealthy choices or breaking the rules. For example, Riley ended up taking the city bus to school several days a week instead of getting a ride from her mom. This one conversation didn't completely heal the rift, but it was a turning point that led to much calmer and more open communication from that point onward.

Planning a Joint Workshop

Last year, I wanted to plan an EOS workshop for midlevel managers. Normally, EOS Implementers like me only work directly with the top leadership team of a company. However, there's value in teaching midlevel managers how EOS works so they can operate better within the system. There was a great opportunity for us to use a beautiful meeting space for free—all I had to do was fill the room with a hundred paying participants.

There are 45 EOS Implementers in New York City, so I thought it would be easy to sell a hundred tickets if each Implementer recommended the workshop to a few of their clients. The workshop would help those clients have more success with EOS, which would make their Implementers and the EOS brand as a whole look good. It seemed like a no-brainer to me.

But when I emailed the 45 EOS Implementers about this, I got pushback. *What's in it for us? Why aren't you sharing the revenue from the tickets we sell? Why are you keeping the whole thing for yourself?*

I was taken aback. I was the first EOS Implementer in New York City. I had created the market all these people were making their living from. I had helped them build their businesses. And now they didn't want to return the favor unless they got paid for it?

That was my immediate, emotional reaction. Instead of responding with that, I prepared an Accusations Audit, brainstorming as many items as I possibly could:

- "You might think promoting this workshop could detract from your own services."

- "You may worry about the time and energy required for promotion not being adequately compensated."
- "You probably question how the workshop's content will surpass what you're already providing."
- "You could be concerned about the implications of participating in a setting with potential client overlap."
- "You might feel overlooked in the promotional and content aspects of the workshop."
- "You may be skeptical about the tangible benefits for your practice beyond the workshop."
- "You could doubt the effectiveness of the postevent engagement strategy for your clients."
- "You might see the requirement for up-front financial investment or effort as disproportionate to the potential returns."
- "You may have reservations about sharing revenue or other forms of financial recognition."
- "You could be uneasy about how success metrics will reflect on your contribution and the value to your clients."

In the end, I didn't deliver this Accusations Audit. My team and I were under time pressure, so we decided to rethink the event for a future date. But just going through the exercise was the perfect way to clear out my negative emotions and get back into a mindset of curiosity.

Winning the Bidding War

An EOS colleague of mine had recently divorced and was looking to buy a new home. His current house sold for a good amount, but he was looking down the barrel of homelessness because the market was so tight in his area—few homes were for sale, prices were high, and there were multiple bidders on every listing. He finally found a property that fit his needs, but when he went to the open house, there were thirty other serious buyers there. He knew he would need to do something special to get this house.

When he talked to the listing agent, he discovered some crucial black swans. The home had belonged to an elderly man who had passed away, and his children were now selling it. It needed substantial repairs and updates, but they were in a rush to get rid of it and didn't want to make the investment. As a result, it had been hard to sell; several serious buyers had backed out when they realized how much work the house needed. The agent told him, "This property has been nothing but trouble, and I just want it gone."

Using this information, we put together an Accusations Audit:

- "You probably think I'm trying to capitalize on the complexities of an estate sale."
- "You might think I'm an investor looking for a quick profit."
- "You may believe I'm a bottom-feeder taking advantage of the situation."
- "You're likely concerned that I'm overestimating the renovation costs, suggesting I'm not serious."
- "You might think we are rushing you into a decision because we've proposed a quick close."
- "You may feel that offering to handle both sides of the commission is too good a deal and reflects desperation."
- "You're probably worried about how quickly all stakeholders can agree to a single course of action."
- "You might be concerned that stakeholders are looking to maximize their piece of the pie, which could conflict with accepting a lower offer."
- "You may think the house is just another listing to me rather than a potential home."

- "You're likely wondering if we are truly prepared to handle the renovations needed."

My colleague used this Accusations Audit to preface a bid that, although it was below the asking price, specifically addressed the sellers' and agent's desires. He proposed to forego the traditional inspection and instead have his trusted contractors look at the property and give him an estimate of renovation costs so they could trust he wouldn't back out over the inspection report. He also proposed a quick closing, with the listing agent handling both sides of the deal—double the commission for her.

That's how, out of a huge pool of bidders, my colleague secured the house—and for $50,000 less than the asking price.

IN SHORT …

- Accusations Audits are *preemptive Labels* that call out your counterpart's possible negative emotions, impressions, assumptions, and dynamics around the situation.
- You *must* use them at the beginning of a conversation, before delivering bad news, and before making an ask. In general, they are useful anytime you're going to say something your counterpart might not want to hear.
- When preparing your Accusations Audits, aim for *overkill*: as many Accusations Audits as possible, as visceral as possible. Overshoot their actual negative emotions.
- Delivering Accusations Audits braces them for bad news. Deliver them one at a time, with plenty of Dynamic Silence in between.
- *Keep going* until they give a clear indication that they're ready to hear what you have to say. Only then can you deliver your bad news or make your ask.

LOW-STAKES PRACTICE

To start getting comfortable with Accusations Audits, do these exercise:

1. **Use in casual apologies.** When apologizing to friends or family for something minor, call out their potential feelings first. For example: "You might think I completely forgot your birthday."
2. **Use before giving constructive feedback.** Before providing feedback to someone, start with an Accusations Audit. For example: "You might think I don't see the good things you've done."
3. **Use with customer service.** When talking to customer service reps, acknowledge their possible frustrations or assumptions. For example: "You might think I'm about to complain and make this difficult for you."
4. **Use in disagreements with friends.** If disagreeing with a friend, use an Accusations Audit to neutralize negative emotions. For example: "You're probably thinking I don't respect your opinion."
5. **Use in low-stakes sales or negotiations.** When negotiating a small deal (like buying something at a flea market), pre-empt the seller's objections. For example: "You're probably thinking I'm trying to undervalue your item."

To learn more about Accusations Audits, scan the QR code and join the Black Swan Community.

CHAPTER 11

TONE

At almost every live training event, Derek does a demonstration called 60 Seconds or She Dies. He chooses three volunteers to play the role of police hostage negotiators, and he plays a robber trapped in a bank with hostages. The negotiators have to call inside the bank and negotiate with the bank robber.

Before the call begins, the negotiators are given some ground rules: They don't know the robber's name. They don't know how many hostages he has. They don't know how many accomplices he has. Most importantly, they are not permitted to negotiate any terms around drugs, alcohol, weapons, ammunition, exchange of hostages, or transportation. Their objective is to get the robber to release the hostages and surrender to the police.

When they get on the phone, Derek says in his most aggressive voice: "Get me a car in sixty seconds or she dies."

He doesn't stop there. He keeps unloading on them in a harsh, rapid-fire tone—making demands and threats, peppering them with insults, and questioning their competence. It's a powerful barrage of verbal attacks.

The outcome is always the same: The negotiators panic and fall apart. They forget all the Black Swan skills they've learned and all the rules they were told to follow. They lie. They threaten him. They negotiate over prohibited items. They pump him for information. Sometimes they even hang up on him.

It's not because they're malicious or stupid. It's because the pressure of the moment makes it impossible to think clearly. They're supremely uncomfortable, and they'll do anything to get comfortable again, up to and including implicitly or explicitly agreeing to provide the hostage taker with a prohibited item.

This exercise vividly illustrates how tone of voice can shape a negotiation. Just by adjusting how you talk, you can make your counterpart dumber or smarter, dial their emotional state up or down. Your tone is one of the most powerful tools at your disposal. Used poorly, it can destroy relationships, blow up deals, and leave nothing but scorched earth behind. But used well, tone will help you build trust, gather information, and lead your counterpart down the path you want them to take.

WHAT IS TONE?

Tone is your nonverbal communication: primarily your voice, supported by your body language and facial expression.

Your tone conveys a huge amount of information. You know this from dealing with text-based communication, which is devoid of tone. You read a message and wonder, *Was that sincere or sarcastic? Excited or annoyed?* That's why we love using emojis so much—they were invented specifically to help us send the right message and avoid being misunderstood.*

When you're on the phone or face-to-face, your tone registers with your counterpart in less than one-tenth of a second—much faster than your words. It tells them how you feel about what you're saying: confident or hesitant, enthusiastic or reluctant, serious or joking, happy or sad. It tells them how you feel about them: respectful or disdainful, curious or uninterested, trusting or skeptical, warm or aloof.

And as you learned from the Law of Negotiation Gravity #3, your tone will trigger an emotional response in your counterpart. A calm, friendly tone will make them relax and open up. A harsh, aggressive tone will make them stress out and close up. An unnatural, insincere, or robotic tone will raise their suspicions. And if there's a disconnect between what you're saying and how you're saying it, they'll believe your tone over your words every time.†

In short, tone can either aid or hinder you in building trust and getting to the truth. It's so powerful that if you're truly listening and using the right tone at the right time, you often don't need any other Tactical Empathy tools at all.

Most people are not consciously aware of their tone most of the time. Sometimes they might not even be perceiving their own tone accurately; what they think they're giving is very different from what their counterpart is receiving. The more skilled you become at deliberately controlling your tone—responding with a thoughtfully chosen tone instead of reactivating with your instinctive tone—the easier it will be to achieve Tactical Empathy with your counterpart.

---

* Arielle Pardes, "The Complete History of Emoji," *Wired*, February 1, 2018, https://www.wired.com/story/guide-emoji/.

† Jessica Stillman, "57 Years Ago, a Legendary Psychologist Discovered the 7-38-55 Rule. It's Still the Secret to Exceptional Emotional Intelligence," *Inc.*, March 29, 2024, https://www.inc.com/jessica-stillman/7-38-55-rule-57-years-old-secret-exceptional-emotional-intelligence.html.

THE THREE TONES

Tone is hard to measure in an absolute way. There's a huge spectrum of elements that combine to create tone: volume, speed, pitch variation, cadence, and more (and that's without even getting into body language). Going down that rabbit hole doesn't serve our purposes; if you can't recognize or enact it intuitively in the moment, it's not helpful.

So, we simplify tone into three basic categories.

The Accommodator Tone is friendly, relaxed, and open.

It's how you talk when you're chatting casually with a friend about something pleasant. It's not overly slow or fast, soft or loud, high or low. It's a nice middle ground with a positive vibe. To be clear, friendly doesn't mean silly or giggly; you can still be serious while making the other person comfortable.

The Accommodator Tone should be your default. Use it at least 80 percent of the time in any given sensitive conversation, particularly when you're in the process of discovering information.

The Analyst Tone is slow, low, and unemotional.

Chris likes to call it the Late-Night FM DJ Voice. Lower the pitch and volume of your voice, enunciate every syllable, and use plenty of pauses. Low and slow. This causes your counterpart's attention to focus sharply.

The Analyst Tone should be used for delivering important information or making an ask. Use it *at most* 20 percent of the time—in the moments when you want to lead your counterpart in a particular direction. It's the most effective way to be concise and direct without offending or hurting the other person.

The Assertive Tone is loud, fast, and intense.

It's the tone you naturally take on when you're worked up about something, in either a positive or a negative way. To you, it feels like you're communicating with passion. To the other person, it feels like you're hostile—maybe even yelling.

The Assertive Tone has *no place* in a sensitive conversation. *Never* use it. If you ever notice yourself using it, take a deep breath and do your best to switch to the Analyst Tone or Accommodator Tone.

You might be surprised that we would take one of the three tones completely off the table, especially if it's your default tone. You might be wondering, Aren't there at least *some* situations where that kind of direct, energetic, pointed communication is appropriate? Actually, yes, there is one: when your goal is to burn your bridges. If you've decided you don't care about building a relationship with your counterpart, by all means, use the Assertive Tone as much as you want.

But if your goal is to achieve Tactical Empathy, the Assertive Tone will do nothing but undermine your efforts. Remember, the very first step on the road to Tactical Empathy is *removing yourself as a threat to your counterpart*. Well, the Assertive Tone amps up your threat factor all over again. The high volume, fast pace, and intense energy cause the other person to put their defensive walls back up, consciously or unconsciously.

Different personalities respond to the Assertive Tone in different ways. Some people (usually those who default to the Assertive Tone themselves) will match it with equal intensity, leading to a shouting match. Others will shut down and withdraw from the conversation. Both are bad outcomes—complete breakdowns in communication.

To sum it all up: Default to the Accommodator Tone. Use the Analyst Tone in the most important and delicate moments. Never use the Assertive Tone.

HOW TO CONTROL YOUR TONE

On paper, that seems pretty easy to understand and remember. The tricky part is actually doing it when you're in the middle of a sensitive conversation. Here are some helpful tips to keep your tone on track.

1. Know your tendencies.

Just by reading the descriptions of the three tones, you probably already have an idea of which one you use most often. We'll dive deeper into this in chapter 15 when we discuss the three Negotiator Personality Types, which correspond to the three tones. Each personality type tends to default to a certain tone, especially when they're under pressure. However, it's crucial to understand that *anyone* can use *any* of the three tones whenever they choose; it's just a matter of staying aware enough to make that conscious choice.

Knowing your tendencies helps boost your awareness. For example, let's say you tend to default to the Analyst Tone, which comes off as cold and aloof if you use it too much or at the wrong times. If you know that about yourself, you know you need to make a conscious effort to use the Accommodator Tone more often, especially at the beginning of the conversation.

2. Smile when you talk.

As we've established, you should be using the Accommodator Tone the vast majority of the time. That tone is positive and friendly, so a great way to get yourself into that mode is to physically smile while you talk. It doesn't have to be goofy or overdone. Just a little smile—the kind of smile you naturally have when you like the person you're talking to and want to make friends with them.

If you're not normally the smiling sort, practice this with a trusted friend. Make sure it's not coming off as fake, creepy, or unnatural—that would defeat the purpose.

3. Stay focused on what's in front of you.

Your inner voice will always betray your outer voice. So if you're distracted by the end game—thinking about what you want out of the interaction—it will come through in your tone. You will start to sound insincere and manipulative, and your counterpart will notice. Stay in the moment and keep making it about them, not you.

4. When you get triggered, slow *way, way, way* down.

We've said it before: In any conversation where negative dynamics are present, accept the fact that you'll get attacked. When that happens, your first instinct is to hit back. You want to make the other person feel the way they just made you feel. Revenge is a powerful motivator.

If you let that instinct win, you'll end up matching assertiveness with assertiveness, and we know where that leads: a shouting match. It's *never* productive, and sometimes it's impossible to recover from. If you want the conversation to actually get somewhere, revenge is the *last* thing you need. As Groucho Marx said, "If you speak when angry, you'll make the best speech you'll ever regret."*

The key to cutting off that unproductive cycle is to *slow down*. People often say you should take a pause or a breath, and that's good, but it's not quite enough. You might take a nice long pause and still come back swinging. Slowing down forces you to keep the brakes on even after you start talking again.

When we say slow down, we mean it literally: Talk. Super. Sloooow. When you're triggered, you're literally dumber; you need to give yourself more time to think, so you can choose your words carefully and avoid saying something you'll regret. Talking slow also helps lower your heart rate, deepen your breathing, and prevent the volume and pitch of your voice from rising. It physically calms you down, even more than just pausing for a few breaths. That in turn encourages your counterpart to calm down as well, so you can both get out of fight-or-flight mode and have a productive conversation.

---

* "Quote Origin: Speak When You're Angry and You'll Make the Best Speech You'll Ever Regret," Quote Investigator, May 17, 2014, https://quoteinvestigator.com/2014/05/17/angry-speech/.

CASE STUDY RESOLUTION

Now that you understand the three tones, it's obvious what Derek is up to in the 60 Seconds or She Dies demonstration. He comes out of the gate with an Assertive Tone to intentionally throw off his counterparts. It works like a charm every time.

But the exercise doesn't end there. Once his poor volunteers have suffered enough of his wrath, he switches to the Analyst Tone: low, slow, and unemotional. He's still asking for the same things; only his tone of voice has changed. The participants know something about the dynamic is different but can't put their finger on it. They're confused, but they're also starting to calm down and listen more closely.

Finally, Derek switches to the Accommodator Tone: relaxed and upbeat, like the friendly neighbor everyone likes to talk to. Again, he's still making the same demands, but his voice has changed. Almost instantly, the negotiators become more cognitively nimble. They can complete a coherent thought, their speech patterns make sense, and they can actually have a two-way dialogue with Derek.

After the exercise, Derek asks if they noticed the tone switching. As Law of Negotiation Gravity #7 predicts, they remember the most intense moment and how it ended—in this case, the Assertive Tone at the beginning and the Accommodator Tone at the end. When Derek asks why they broke the rules—why they lied to him, threatened him, et cetera—all they can say is that they couldn't think of anything else in that moment. His tone hijacked their brains. It put them in fight-or-flight mode, where even the most intelligent people can't respond rationally. Then, just by changing how he talked—*without* changing his demands—Derek was able to pull them back out of that threatened state and into a productive conversation.

MORE REAL-WORLD EXAMPLES

Tone is just as powerful in the real world as it is in Derek's training exercise. Here are some true stories of tone in action.

Black Swan IP

The Black Swan Group was in a negotiation over IP with another company that wanted to collaborate with us. They were a publicly traded Fortune 500 company, accustomed to bullying their vendors to get their way. We made it clear that we didn't do work for hire; any agreement would have to give us ownership over what we created. However, after we thought this was well established, our counterpart brought it up again.

At that point, Chris wanted to drive the message home in the most direct and serious way. So, he switched to the Analyst Tone—low, slow, and unemotional.

"We … do not … do work … for hire."

There was no mistaking his message: If they asked again, we were out. But because he didn't yell or get upset, there was no damage done on either side. Even if the deal hadn't worked out in the end, the relationship would have been preserved.

The Triggered Receptionist

One day at the dentist, I got some bad news: a cavity! It would need to be filled, but I would have to come back another day for that.

When I went to the front desk to check out and schedule the filling, the receptionist seemed to be trying to rush me out of the office. I was surprised—the dentist had said he would tell the receptionist to schedule my filling before I left. That's when I made the mistake of saying, "Didn't they tell you I need to have my cavity filled?"

She did *not* like that. She was already in a bad mood, and my question not only put another task on her plate but also implied—in her mind—that she wasn't doing her job right. Her attitude soured even more.

Instead of scheduling the appointment, she told me she was going to send me an estimate of costs. I reminded her that I had dental insurance, and she snapped at me, "I know you have insurance."

I was so thrown off by her tone that I just gave up and left without scheduling my filling. It wasn't until I got home that my mind was calm enough to realize what was really going on in that conversation. By going through my insurance, the dentist would get paid less than if I paid out of pocket. Not only that, but working with my insurance was a hassle for the receptionist: She had to request a prior authorization from the insurance company first, and the payment for the procedure would take a long time to come through. It would be better for her and her employer if I paid out of pocket and applied for the insurance reimbursement myself.

I couldn't make that logical leap when I was at the office because her tone made it so hard for me to think. I'm an obsessive student and practitioner of Tactical Empathy, and yet I was still triggered and compromised by someone else's Assertive Tone.

IN SHORT ...

- Tone is your nonverbal communication: your body language, your facial expression, and above all, your voice.
- Your tone will trigger an emotional response in your counterpart (Law of Negotiation Gravity #3).
- There are three kinds of Tone:
    - The Accommodator Tone is friendly, relaxed, and open. This is your default—use it at least 80 percent of the time.
    - The Analyst Tone is slow, low, and unemotional. Use it less than 20 percent of the time, to deliver an important message or make an ask.
    - The Assertive Tone is loud, fast, and intense. It feels threatening to your counterpart, so you should *never* use it in a sensitive conversation.
- To maintain the right tone, it helps to know your tendencies, smile when you talk, and stay focused on what's in front of you. If you get triggered, slow *way* down to avoid slipping into the Assertive Tone.

LOW-STAKES PRACTICE

To start getting comfortable with Tone, do these exercises.

1. **Practice an easygoing and approachable tone.** Smile when you talk, and your voice will follow. Use this calm, agreeable voice to de-escalate tension in minor conflicts, such as deciding what movie to watch. Notice how it changes the dynamic.
2. **Practice a low and slow tone.** Deliberately lower your volume, lower your pitch, and enunciate each syllable. Use this voice to project seriousness and resolve to family and friends when you're setting boundaries, saying no, or making an ask.
3. **Reflect on the impact of a harsh tone.** Think back to a time when you got triggered and used an aggressive tone. What impact did that have on your mental and emotional state? What impact did it have on your counterpart's state? What effect did it have on the overall communication? (A great place to see this in action is on *Shark Tank*. Watch the show, listen for the Assertive Tone, and see how it affects the person on the receiving end.)

To learn more about Tone, scan the QR code and join the Black Swan Community.

CHAPTER 12

CALIBRATED QUESTIONS

One of my EOS clients is a construction company, and at one point last year, they ran into some serious cash flow problems. They were having trouble getting paid by the general contractor on a big project, and as a result, they failed to pay a big bill to one of their suppliers on time. In total, they owed the supplier $600,000, of which $247,000 was past due.

The supplier was, understandably, not happy and threatened to stop fulfilling their orders until the account was paid. This would have been a big problem for my client, because it would cause delays in their work and potentially make it even harder for them to get paid. Ultimately, it could have even put them out of business. They had some creative ideas for solving the problem with minimal pain for everyone involved, but how could they get their supplier on board? After all, the supplier was already angry and didn't have much to lose by cutting them off.

If you've been paying attention, you've probably already guessed that this is a good situation for an Accusations Audit. My client had to deliver bad news *and* make an ask, both of which are perfect circumstances for that tool. However, they would also need another tool—one that would help their supplier collaborate with them and buy into their solution.

That's precisely what Calibrated Questions are for.

WHAT ARE CALIBRATED QUESTIONS?

> *Calibrated Questions are open-ended questions— usually starting with "what" or "how"—designed to make your counterpart think and solve problems.*

For example:

- "How would you like to proceed?"
- "What do you see as the next step?"
- "How do we avoid that problem?"
- "What should I do if that happens?"

We use "what" and "how" because those are the questions most likely to provoke and shape deeper thoughts, moving the conversation forward. "Who" and "when" don't reveal much, and "why" can too easily come across as an attack—it makes people feel like they're being asked to defend their choices against the judgment of the asker. (In fact, you should *never* ask why except in a very specific situation that we'll discuss in chapter 16.)

When The Black Swan Group originally started testing the concept of Calibrated Questions, the intent was to draw out information. However, we learned over time that direct questioning breeds resistance more often than not. If I ask you a bunch of what and how questions, you know I'm trying to get information, and you know that giving me information makes you vulnerable and threatened. Before long, you're deflecting and doing your best *not* to answer my questions. That's why we taught you (in chapter 6) to gather information using Labels instead of questions.

Calibrated Questions now serve a different purpose: to shape the thinking of the counterpart. Think of it like the Socratic method; as Socrates said, "I cannot teach anybody anything. I can only make them think." What he meant was that true learning doesn't happen when an idea is presented to a person. It only happens when that person goes through the thought process to discover the idea themselves, firsthand.

The same is true of solving problems in a negotiation. You come in with a solution in mind, but if you simply present it to your counterpart, they will resist it or reject it outright. However, if you guide their thinking so they feel like they came up with the solution themselves, they're much more likely to adopt it. By encouraging them to think critically, you increase the chances of both sides reaching an agreement and actually following through on it.

In effect, Calibrated Questions allow you to give the other side the illusion of being in control while retaining the upper hand yourself. It's a bit like keeping a lion in captivity. If it's in a fifty-acre park that's fenced in, the lion has the illusion of control over this vast area, but you are still setting the parameters.

WHEN TO USE A CALIBRATED QUESTION

In general, Calibrated Questions are useful whenever you want to shape your counterpart's thinking. Here are some examples of when and how that might happen in a sensitive conversation.

1. To guide a problem-solving or decision-making process

In any sensitive conversation—whether it's a sales call, a merger discussion, or a spat with your spouse—what you want is to influence what the other person decides to do. However, even in situations where you're supposed to be advising the other person (e.g., they're your client, your student, your child, etc.), they don't always want to follow your advice.

If you just tell your counterpart what you think they should do, their first instinct is to resist.

This is the perfect situation for a Calibrated Question. If you are at the point in the conversation where you are shaping thought or problem-solving, you have already poured heavy doses of Tactical Empathy into the interaction. You have done the work of removing yourself as a threat and making the other person feel understood. Even if you're "on their side," this is still the essential first step. If you skip it, their defenses will be up and they will not be open to your influence. So before you even think about Calibrated Questions, take the time to listen closely, learn as much as possible about their thoughts and feelings, and articulate those things back to them.

Then comes the moment for Calibrated Questions. You can use them to guide your counterpart's thinking throughout the problem-solving and decision-making process.

Clearly state the problem:

- What is the core issue here?
- What are the biggest challenges we face?
- What is the limiting factor?

Focus on the stakes at hand:

- What happens if we do nothing?
- What happens if we fail?
- What happens if you do X?

Come up with a solution or make a decision:

- How would you like to proceed?
- What's the next best step?

This is so powerful because it allows them to preserve their autonomy. As we said earlier, it gives them the illusion of control. You're not telling them what to do; you're trusting them to make the decision on their own. And because you're not putting them in a defensive position, they are open to considering your view on the situation.

2. To ensure implementation of an agreement

You learned in chapter 4 that there's always a team of deal-killers on the other side (Law of Negotiation Gravity #10). Calibrated Questions are the perfect tool for addressing that issue and prompting your counterpart to think through their response to the deal-killers ahead of time.

- "What will others in your organization think?"
- "What will you say to them to help allay their concerns?"
- "How can I help you with that conversation?"
- "How will I know we're on track with our agreement?"
- "What should we do if we find ourselves off track?"
- "If I haven't heard from you by our agreed-upon deadline, what should my next move be?"

3. To travel back in time

Let's say your counterpart agrees to do X by Y date. That date comes and goes … and nothing. To address that misalignment between what they said and what they did, you can use a Calibrated Question to take them back in time to the moment they made the promise:

- "When you said I would have X by Y date, what should my expectations have been?"
- "When you said I would have X by Y date, what did that mean to you?"

4. To start the conversation when you have no information

Sometimes, you go into a conversation with little or no context—for example, if you're a service provider meeting with a potential new client for the first time, or a teacher talking with a student who has requested a meeting. All you know is that they want to talk with you. They haven't yet told you anything about their circumstances or what they want.

In this situation, one particular Calibrated Question is a good conversation opener: "How can I help you?" or "What can I do for you?"

This immediately reduces your threat factor; it shows that you're there to listen to their agenda, not push yours. That encourages your counterpart to jump in and start giving you information. Right off the bat, you're well on your way to getting to the truth.

My godfather was vice chairman at a major Wall Street firm, and this question was the first thing out of his mouth every single time he answered the phone, because it saved him time and helped him cut to the chase. As an EOS Implementer, I use this question to start virtually every sales call. The black swans come out immediately—they tell me exactly what they're struggling with in their business, what their goals are, what's keeping them up at night, and what's getting in their way. Typically, the response is a rambling stream of all of their challenges, fears, obstacles, and hopes—and I just met them five seconds ago. They give me everything I need to make them feel understood and build their trust in my ability to help solve their problems.

PITFALLS OF CALIBRATED QUESTIONS

Calibrated Questions are an extremely flexible, versatile tool that's useful in many different situations. There are really only a couple of ways to trip up when using them.

1. Don't weaponize your questions.

As we said way back in chapter 2, tools are just tools, and they can be used for good or evil. With the wrong intent (and remember, humans can smell intent), a question can easily become a weapon—an accusation, an insult, or a "gotcha." For example:

- "How does that (not) make sense?"
- "How could you possibly know that?"
- "What makes your suggestion the best?"
- "What experience do you have with this kind of thing?"

Be very careful of asking Calibrated Questions when you're feeling negative toward your counterpart. When a question comes from a place of fear or anger, or it's about you and not them, your counterpart will pick up on it no matter how carefully you try to moderate your tone. They'll get defensive in return, and you cannot make any real progress from that position.

That's why you must always ask Calibrated Questions from a place of genuine curiosity. As with Labels, check yourself—can you taste how good the words will feel coming out of your mouth? If so, you probably shouldn't say them.

2. Be careful with "How am I supposed to do that?"

This particular Calibrated Question featured prominently in *Never Split the Difference*. It was a response Chris used when hostage-taking counterparts demanded something he couldn't give. The intention behind it was to guide his counterpart to think in terms of reality.

Years later, we realized that many readers were treating this question like a silver bullet. They would use it at completely inappropriate moments and end up sounding like a manipulative bully. So, we want to address this directly now.

This Calibrated Question is the first Phase of No (more on this in chapter 14). It should only be used as a *last-ditch effort* to salvage the conversation when you're at an impasse. If you use it too early, when you're not at an impasse but you just want the other side to back off, it will come off as hostile. If you're using all the Black Swan skills at your disposal, you should never need this question because you should never reach an impasse.

If you do have to use it, your counterpart's response will tell you if they're serious about reaching an agreement. If they are, this question will get them to rethink their approach and start negotiating with themselves. If, on the other hand, they say something like, "That's your problem," that's a sign that most likely they have been pushed as far as they can go. Now you have a decision to make: Accept the deal in front of you or walk away.

CASE STUDY RESOLUTION

Now that you understand how Calibrated Questions work, let's see how they fit into the story of our cash-strapped construction company. As we mentioned, the first step in the conversation was an Accusations Audit. That's not our main focus here, but just for fun, let's take a look at some of the Audits they came up with:

- "You probably think we are not managing our finances effectively."
- "You might believe this delay indicates a deeper issue in our operations."
- "You may think that we are not prioritizing your payments."
- "You are probably wondering if we can meet any payment commitments."
- "We probably appear disorganized and unreliable right now."

Now, the construction company had some potential solutions to the payment problem in mind. However, presenting those solutions directly was not the ideal move. They were not in a position to be asking for favors, and the supplier was far less likely to buy into a solution imposed from the outside than one they had come up with themselves. So, before entering the conversation, we came up with a list of Calibrated Questions to guide the problem-solving process:

- "What are we trying to accomplish with this payment extension?"
- "How is maintaining our supply relationship worthwhile for both of us?"
- "What's the core issue behind the urgency of the payment?"
- "How does this payment delay affect your operations?"
- "How does this fit into your overall financial objectives?"
- "How does this situation affect the rest of your team?"
- "How on board are your colleagues with finding a solution?"
- "What do your colleagues see as their main challenges in this area?"
- "What are we up against in finding a mutually agreeable solution?"
- "What is the biggest challenge you face in granting an extension?"

These Calibrated Questions sparked a collaborative discussion that led to a satisfactory solution for everyone. Beyond that, they uncovered solutions we had not even considered, ones even more favorable than we initially thought possible. The supplier agreed to reduce the amount due immediately, extend the payment terms, and continue delivering materials without interruption. Plus, they offered to use their relationships to help the construction company accelerate payment from the general contractor who was dragging their feet. This was a huge relief for my client, and it led to an even *better* working relationship with their supplier than before.

MORE REAL-WORLD EXAMPLES
The Walmart Deal-Killers
One of my clients provides a very unique service: They capture birds that have become trapped in large warehouse stores. Walmart is one of their clients, but they aren't hired directly by the national corporate people. They're hired by local and regional managers, who then have to get approval for the expense from their corporate superiors.

That means every time they go into a sales conversation with a new store, they know there's a team of deal-killers waiting in the wings at corporate. To mitigate that risk, they rely on Calibrated Questions. First, they share a simple graphic that shows their proven process—a step-by-step explanation of exactly what they do and why it's so effective. They give this document to their counterpart to share with their team.

Then they say something like, "I know you have to run this by corporate to get it approved. You've told me that you feel confident that we will solve your problem, but they might have doubts. What will you say to allay their fears?"

Without fail, the managers are able to articulate my client's value proposition clearly, thanks in large part to the proven process graphic. That helps everyone—my client *and* his counterpart—walk away with confidence that the deal will go through.

An Alarming Visit
Last year, a friend of mine (let's call him David) hosted a weeklong visit from his brother and his mother. This was a big deal because the brother hadn't been to any family events in years. He was something of a "free spirit," and his beliefs and lifestyle tended to clash with the rest of the family.

One day at about 4:00 a.m., they heard the fire alarm of the house turn on, then quickly off again. A minute later, it happened again—on, then off. David got up and checked all the rooms of the house for signs of fire. When he got to the room where his brother was staying, he found his brother wide awake. David had his suspicions—his brother had been known to smoke from time to time—but he didn't want to start a fight at 4:00 a.m., so he just went back to bed.

Later, he asked my advice on how to approach the conversation without reopening a family rift that seemed to be on the mend. As with any situation where you have to tell someone something they don't want to hear, I advised starting with an Accusations Audit: "You're probably going to feel like I'm being judgmental …" "It seems like coming to be with the family makes you anxious …" and so on. Then, instead of interrogating the brother about whether he had been smoking in the house, I advised using Labels to invite him to tell his side of the story. "It sounds like we did something that made you think it was OK to smoke in the house."

Once the facts were all out on the table, David needed to use Calibrated Questions to solve the problem collaboratively with his brother. "What are you going to do to make sure your smoking doesn't affect us or our home?" Calibrated Questions could also be useful to make sure this didn't cause another rift between the brothers. "Going forward, how will I know that we as brothers are OK?"

IN SHORT …

- Calibrated Questions are open-ended questions—usually starting with "what" or "how"—designed to make your counterpart think and solve problems.
- Their purpose is not to gather information but to shape your counterpart's thinking.
- Use Calibrated Questions when you want to guide the problem-solving or decision-making process, ensure implementation of an agreement, or start the conversation when you have no information.
- Be very careful with your delivery. Questions can easily come across as invasive or accusatory, especially if your counterpart

is already in a negative state. Use the Accommodator Tone, and never pose a question with the intention to punish, embarrass, or otherwise undercut your counterpart.

LOW-STAKES PRACTICE

To start getting comfortable with Calibrated Questions, do these exercises.

1. **Test agreements with Calibrated Questions.** When someone agrees to something small (e.g., your child agrees to finish their homework before dinner), practice testing that agreement with "what" and "how" questions. For example: "What will you do to make sure you finish on time?"
2. **Use Calibrated Questions to invoke fear of loss.** When you're helping a friend or family member think through a problem or make a decision, use "what" and "how" questions to get them thinking about what they stand to lose. For example: "How will things look in a month if you don't make a change now?"
3. **Start conversations with a Calibrated Question.** Instead of starting with your own agenda, ask, "How can I help you?" or "What can I do for you?" Notice how this impacts your counterpart's demeanor.

To learn more about Calibrated Questions, scan the QR code and join the Black Swan Community.

CHAPTER 13

ENCOURAGERS

Welcome to the shortest chapter in the book! This skill is so intuitive and self-explanatory that you don't even need a story to illustrate it. So, we'll get right to the point.

WHAT ARE ENCOURAGERS?

Encouragers are words, sounds, and gestures that indicate you're listening and urge your counterpart to go on.

They keep the conversation flowing and make the speaker feel heard and valued. They also help you stay engaged as a listener. Using an Encourager is just one more little swing of the Tactical Empathy ax.

For example:

- "Uh-huh."
- "Hmm."

- "Right."
- "Really?"
- "OK."
- "That makes sense."
- "Oh?"
- "Interesting."
- "Exactly."
- "Is that so?"
- "Got it."
- "Absolutely."
- "Indeed."
- Nodding, facial expressions, and other body language

You're probably thinking, *I do this all the time!* That's right—virtually everyone does, without even thinking about it. So you can relax; this is the one Tactical Empathy skill you're already an expert at.

That said, there are certain common phrases that may seem like good Encouragers but are not. These fall into two categories.

First, avoid anything that shifts the focus from your counterpart to you by using "I." For example:

- "I'm with you."
- "I hear you."
- "I understand."
- "I see."

Remember, it's not about you—it's about them. Using "I" subtly undermines your efforts to make them feel understood.

Second, avoid any kind of explicit prompt for your counterpart to say more. For example:

- "Go on."
- "Please continue."

- "Tell me more."
- "Let's unpack that."

Counterintuitively, these phrases can make it seem like you're *not* listening very well or you're impatient and rushing them to get to the point. If your counterpart has just given you a lot of information and you say something like this, they'll wonder what more you could possibly want. If they've been tight-lipped, it will sound like you're prying for information they don't want to give. If you ever feel tempted to say these phrases, reach for an alternative—a different Encourager, or even better, a Label or Summary that demonstrates you've heard what the other person has already said.

WHEN TO USE ENCOURAGERS

There are no set rules about exactly when or how to use Encouragers. Their only purpose is to keep your counterpart talking and show that you're still paying attention, so they can fit in naturally at almost any point in the conversation. Most of the time, you'll intuitively use them correctly without even recognizing that you're doing it. In fact, most people find that the less they think about it, the better they are at it.

That said, here are two pieces of advice about timing your use of Encouragers.

1. Don't interrupt your counterpart.

If they're already on a roll, throwing in an Encourager can actually throw them off. Eye contact, tilting of the head, and a smile will suffice. Using Encouragers too soon during a phone call is especially problematic. They might mistake your Encourager for an indication that you want to say something. They might lose the rhythm or their train of thought and have trouble getting back into the groove of what they were saying. So when your counterpart's words are flowing, just let them flow, no encouragement necessary.

2. Encourage when they look for it.

Throughout the conversation, your counterpart will instinctively be checking for signs that you're listening. They'll look at you to see whether you're watching and what your face is doing; they'll pause in a monologue to see if you're with them. Those are the perfect moments for Encouragers. They're actively looking for confirmation that you're paying attention, so give it to them.

PITFALLS OF ENCOURAGERS

Again, most people use Encouragers perfectly well without thinking about it at all. However, there are a few mistakes that can cause Encouragers to sound unnatural and off-putting. Here's what you want to avoid.

1. Overdoing it

Using too many Encouragers makes you sound fake. It gives the impression that you're working really hard to *seem* like a great listener without actually *being* one. As we keep saying, people can smell intent. If you're focused on using Encouragers instead of actually listening to your counterpart, they can tell—and they won't like it.

2. Lack of variety

Be careful of leaning too heavily on any one Encourager. If you were speaking, how would it feel to get seven "uh-huh"s in a row from your counterpart? Or "got it" every other sentence? It makes you feel like the person is fake, distracted, or bored—and that's especially true if you're on the phone and can't see each other's faces.

For most people, this isn't an issue. However, some people do end up repeatedly using the same Encourager, either because they're thinking too hard or they've simply fallen into the habit. A little awareness is all it takes to cure this problem. Remember, Tactical Empathy is like conversational seasoning—variety is important, and you don't want to overdo any one thing.

3. Mismatched energy

In any sensitive conversation, you'll be much more successful if you match your counterpart's energy. If they're upbeat and positive about what they're saying, your Encouragers should feel upbeat and positive. If they're serious and thoughtful, you should be too. If you're genuinely tuned in to the other person and what they're saying, this should happen naturally; humans are hardwired to mirror each other's emotions. That's why mismatched energy is such a problem: It indicates to your counterpart that you're not really paying attention to them, which makes your Encouragers sound fake.

IN SHORT ...

- Encouragers are words, sounds, and gestures that indicate you're listening and urge your counterpart to go on.
- Most people do this naturally without thinking about it. In fact, the more you think about it, the more likely it is to sound forced and unnatural. The most important thing is to genuinely listen to your counterpart.
- Use Encouragers when your counterpart pauses or appears to be checking in to see if you're following their train of thought. Be careful not to interrupt them.
- Use variety, don't overdo it, and match your counterpart's energy.

LOW-STAKES PRACTICE

Most people are already comfortable with Encouragers, but there are still a few exercises you can do to hone your use of this tool.

1. **Replace "I" statements with neutral Encouragers.** Pay attention and notice if you tend to use statements like "I'm

with you," "I hear you," or "I see." Try to catch yourself and replace those phrases with Encouragers that don't redirect the focus to you.

2. **Replace explicit invitations to say more.** Similarly, notice if you're in the habit of saying things like "Go on," "Tell me more," or "Let's unpack that." Again, try to catch yourself and use a neutral Encourager instead.

3. **Test how far Encouragers can go.** When chatting with a barista, rideshare driver, or store clerk, see how long you can keep them talking using only Encouragers (verbal *and* nonverbal).

To learn more about Encouragers, scan the QR code and join the Black Swan Community.

CHAPTER 14

"I" MESSAGES AND THE PHASES OF NO

At Black Swan training events, it's not uncommon for there to be at least one person in the room who is determined to prove to everyone how smart they are. They've read our books a thousand times, attended our online courses, and watched our MasterClass course, and they think they know everything. They pretend they've come to the event to learn, when really they've come to get our attention.

This happened to a particularly obnoxious degree at an event last year. One participant just would not stop with the constant stream of comments and show-off "questions." The lead coach of the session, Troy—one of the kindest and most patient people in the world—could barely make it through his presentation. He was about to lose it with this guy, and so was everyone else in the room.

You might be thinking, *Just throw him out—if he's disrupting the learning process for others, he's gotta go.* That was certainly tempting, but it wasn't the smartest move. This guy had paid thousands of dollars to be there. If we maintained a good relationship, he would probably be worth thousands more to the company in the future. On the other hand, if we turned this event into a bad experience for him, he would probably give negative feedback that could damage our reputation. Plus, our credibility was at risk—it wouldn't look so good for the experts to lose their cool and fail to use the Black Swan skills in front of a hundred people.

So, what could we do to stop the interruptions without making him feel attacked? We need tools for being assertive without being aggressive—and that's exactly what "I" Messages and the Phases of No are for.

WHAT IS AN "I" MESSAGE?

> *An "I" Message is a technique for confronting persistent counterproductive behavior without sounding accusatory.*

It's a means for setting healthy boundaries, allowing you to directly address the issue while letting your counterpart save face. For example:

- "**When you** continuously throw out ultimatums, **I feel** like I'm backed into a corner **because** you're limiting the options we have for moving forward."
- "**When you** refuse to entertain any of my ideas for resolution, **I feel** the situation is hopeless **because** agreement seems out of reach."
- "**When you** continue to ask me for work outside the scope of the contract, **I feel** concerned **because** I'm not sure how we're going to continue this business relationship in a healthy way."

This is a *very* assertive move to make in a conversation. That's why we saved it for last—so you're (hopefully) not tempted to take it on before you fully understand what Tactical Empathy is about and what other tools are available to you.

That said, there will be times when you're dealing with a counterpart who repeatedly engages in counterproductive behavior—raising their voice, canceling meetings at the last minute, interrupting others, not paying on time, et cetera. Failure to address that behavior impedes your ability to influence. And as we said at the very beginning of this book, Tactical Empathy is *not* meant to turn you into a doormat. In fact, it makes it easier to be assertive—and to do so effectively, without starting a fight.

That's what the "I" Message is for: to tell your counterpart to knock it off and actually get them to agree to do so. It identifies the problem without placing blame, then focuses them on what they stand to lose if they don't cease and desist. Remember Law of Negotiation Gravity #1: Fear of loss is the single biggest driver of human decision-making and behavior.

HOW TO DELIVER AN "I" MESSAGE

As you probably noticed from the examples, an "I" Message has a very specific structure: "When you _____, I feel _____ because _____."

You might have seen something like this before. It's commonly used in psychology, with a slightly different structure: "I feel _____ when you _____ because _____."

We've tweaked this in two important ways. First, we flip the first two parts so the statement is leading with a focus on your counterpart instead of you. Sequence matters; before you talk about yourself, talk about them and their behavior. Second, the "because" shouldn't be just anything; it should focus your counterpart's attention on what they stand to lose if they don't change their behavior.

For example: "When you continue to ask for work outside the scope of the contract, I feel frustrated ..." A good way to finish that sentence would be "... because I'm not sure how we can continue our partnership in a healthy way." A not-so-effective alternative would be "... because now I have to go back to my people and explain the changes you want." You having to go back to your people doesn't cost your counterpart anything, so it doesn't motivate them to change their behavior.

Because the "I" Message is an assertive move, and your counterpart might not like what you're about to say, you should set it up with an Accusations Audit:

- "This is probably going to take you off guard ..."
- "You're going to think I'm being too sensitive ..."
- "You're going to wonder why I'm bringing this up now ..."
- And so on

Then, deliver your "I" Message: "When you repeatedly cancel our calls at the last minute, I feel frustrated because I don't know how we can continue this relationship if you don't respect my time."

Follow your "I" Message with Dynamic Silence. The silence is crucial; this is a punch in the face, and you want to let it land. Let them feel it and stew in it. Don't be the one to break the silence.

If they break the silence with an apology, you're good. If they break it with more counterproductive behavior, get curious. What's the message this behavior is sending you? Are they crying out for you to notice some crucial thing that you've missed? Or are they just trying to hurt or manipulate you?

This is a judgment call moment. Do you want to continue subjecting yourself to this behavior, or are you going to exit the situation?

Sometimes—in a family relationship, for example—exiting the situation isn't an option. In that case, give them more Dynamic Silence to see if they'll calm down, apologize, and own up to the issue. Then, use Calibrated Questions to invite them to collaborate on a solution to the problem. For example: "What concrete steps will you take to prevent this from happening again?" With patience and repeated applications of the Tactical Empathy tools, you should be able to make progress even with the most difficult people.

WHEN TO USE AN "I" MESSAGE

In any sensitive conversation, there's a good chance the other side will do something to tick you off. Do not—we repeat, *do not*—immediately jump to an "I" Message. This is a tool of last resort, designed for dealing with *persistent* bad behavior.

If it's a first-time offense, you're not ready for an "I" Message. Instead, get curious. Use the other Black Swan skills—Labels, Mirrors, Summaries, Dynamic Silence, et cetera—to try to uncover what's driving the behavior. Chances are pretty good that it's not malicious; they're probably not intentionally trying to attack you or take advantage of you. There's some other explanation for what you're seeing, and getting to that truth will allow you to handle the issue without getting assertive.

However, if the problematic behavior happens *three or more times* and is interfering with your ability to move the conversation forward, it's time to address it head-on. Remember that your goal is not to punish your counterpart. It's to get them to agree to change their behavior so you get back to having a productive dialogue.

PITFALLS OF "I" MESSAGES

1. Punching back

Be *very* careful: The "I" Message is the closest thing to a verbal weapon that you'll find in this book. Given that you're responding to repeated counterproductive behavior, you're almost certainly feeling pretty negative about your counterpart. The temptation to punch back will be strong—probably stronger in this moment than at any other time.

Rein in that instinct. If at all possible, take a break from the conversation to cool off and shift into a mindset of curiosity before you deliver your "I" Message. This is already an extremely assertive move, and if it crosses the line into an attack, it could easily backfire on you.

2. Using the wrong tone

The only appropriate tone for an "I" Message is the Analyst Tone: low, slow, and unemotional. You need to convey that you're deadly serious without threatening them. The Accommodator Tone is too gentle and easy to brush off for this scenario. The Assertive Tone—although tempting at this moment—is too aggressive and hostile. Only the Analyst Tone allows you to take a hard line without triggering your counterpart.

3. Using it too soon

We've said it already, but it bears repeating: Do *not* use an "I" Message too soon. Wait for the counterproductive behavior to become persistent. As Derek says, the first time is happenstance, the second time is coincidence, and the third time is enemy action. Unless the same bad behavior has happened three or more times, you're not ready for an "I" Message.

4. Not using it when it's called for

On the flip side, some people are afraid to use an "I" Message when they really need to. (This is especially true of the Accommodator personality type, as you'll learn in chapter 15.) If you let yourself get smacked around for too long without setting clear boundaries, your resentment toward your counterpart will just build and build. Let it go on too long, and they'll eventually push you past your breaking point and you'll explode. Once that happens, there may be no salvaging the conversation or the relationship. Better to draw your line in the sand well before that point, using an "I" Message.

5. Not leveraging fear of loss

We said earlier that the "because" part of your statement should speak to what your counterpart stands to lose if they don't quit it. However, people often forget to do this when crafting their "I" Messages. They end up with a statement that speaks to their own pain but doesn't have much impact on their counterpart. If you really want to motivate someone to do something—especially something they don't want to do, like changing their behavior—you've got to appeal to their fear of loss. They might not be moved by your suffering, or even by the prospect of some gain, but you can bet that a potential loss of something that matters to them will get their attention.

6. Not practicing ahead of time

This is one of the most difficult Black Swan skills. It's nuanced, it's assertive, and you have to use it in a delicate moment, when emotions are running high on both sides. You have a much better chance of success if you think it through and practice it out loud ahead of time, with a friend or in the mirror. If you've noticed the same bad behavior repeated twice, go ahead and prepare your "I" Message. Make sure you know exactly what you're going to say and how to deliver it. Then, if the behavior happens a third time, you'll be ready for it.

THE FOUR PHASES OF NO

One of the most important uses of assertiveness in a negotiation is in saying no to an agreement. There are times when you and your counterpart simply cannot agree on how to move forward, but it can be hard to say no without offending them—especially when they really don't want to take no for an answer. When that happens, here's how to show that you're willing to walk away without actually threatening to walk away (which could offend them and blow up the deal).

Phase 1: "How am I supposed to do that?"

This is a Calibrated Question we first mentioned in chapter 12 by way of warning. Like all the tools in this chapter, use it with caution, only when it is truly warranted. Don't throw it into the conversation whenever you hear something you don't like. This question is reserved for when you genuinely do not see a way forward—when you are ready to walk away from the deal unless their terms change.

Try this question at least twice. In many cases, you'll get a little movement from your counterpart the first time. Hopefully, they will put themselves in your shoes, see what a difficult position you're in, and give a little to save the agreement. The second or third time, they'll confirm that you've pushed as far as they're willing to go. If the terms are still unacceptable to you, it's time for the next Phase of No.

Phase 2: "That just doesn't work for us."

This is a gentle but firm indication that you're not moving another inch. You're ready to walk away. It's the next degree of assertiveness, which may motivate your counterpart to offer additional concessions. That might be enough to bring the agreement together, in which case, great. However, they may also continue pushing you to reconsider your stance, which you're not willing to do. In that case, move to the next Phase of No.

Phase 3: "I can't do that."

This sentence kicks up the assertiveness one more notch. No excuses or explanations, just a simple statement that you cannot accept what they're offering. In most cases, this is enough to end the conversation. However, if your counterpart is highly emotionally invested in getting a deal done, they may continue to try to persuade you. That's when you move to the final Phase of No.

Phase 4: "No."

It can't get any clearer. If they pushed you all the way here, there's nothing else left to say.

In all four Phases of No, the delivery is everything. The goal is to be assertive *without* coming across as aggressive, hostile, dismissive, disrespectful, or offensive in any way. Remember, this deal may not work out today but this person could be valuable to you later. Your delivery at this moment can make or break the future of the relationship.

There are three things you need to do to deliver this "no" message successfully.

Stick with the Analyst Tone.

Remember, low, unemotional, and slow—very slow. This focuses their attention and shows that what you're saying is vitally important. The Accommodator Tone is too casual for this serious moment, and again, the Assertive Tone is never a good idea. Analyst is the way to go.

Brace them for what you're about to say.

Start with an apology or a mini Accusations Audit to soften the blow. These are just a few examples—use whatever feels right to you in your context.

- "I'm sorry, but how am I supposed to do that?"
- "I'm afraid that just doesn't work for us."
- "This is gonna suck … I can't do that."
- "I apologize, but no."

Follow your assertion with Dynamic Silence.

Give the other side all the time they need to digest what you've said. Jumping in to say more before they can respond will only work against you. Wait patiently to hear what they're thinking.

Follow those three rules, and you can hold your ground like a brick wall without offending the other side. This is especially effective with salespeople who have been trained in aggressive tactics like "yes momentum," which has been popular in sales since the 1980s and says that if you can get someone to say yes three times, you're far more likely to make the sale. Most people don't know how to push back on those tactics. If you do, you will catch them off guard. In many cases, they are very reluctant to lose the deal and will make concessions to keep you at the table.

CASE STUDY RESOLUTION

Now that you've learned how to be assertive without being aggressive, let's go back to the heckler at the Black Swan training event. To get him in line without leaving him feeling insulted and cheated, we needed a carefully calibrated "I" Message.

Full disclosure: That's not actually what we did. During the session, all the coaches were so stuck in our feelings—frustration, anger, indignation—that we weren't thinking clearly. Despite being a group of Tactical Empathy experts, we were so triggered that it didn't occur to any of us to use an "I" Message. Personally, I wanted to just kick the heckler out, but I knew that was a bad idea. Instead, I gave him some kind of clumsily worded warning that if he kept interrupting, he'd be gone.

Later that day, when we had all calmed down, one of the other coaches realized our mistake. She came up with the perfect "I" Message that Troy could have used immediately after the session: "When you continually interrupt the flow of the class, I feel frustrated because I don't know if it's a smart move to allow you to stay for the rest of the day." That would have let the heckler know that he was at risk of being kicked out of the event, without having to actually make that threat. Most likely, there would have been no more interruptions after that, and the relationship would have been undamaged.

MORE REAL-WORLD EXAMPLES

Broken Payment Promises

My usual deal with clients is that they pay me on or before the day of the session. However, I have one client who pays on Fridays even though we have sessions on Tuesdays, because of how their payment system works. I agreed to this arrangement, but even after being given this concession, they kept paying me late. When I asked about it, I could never seem to get a straight answer about when the payment would come through.

So, I started with an Accusations Audit:

- "You're going to think I'm running out of money in my bank account …"
- "You're going to think I'm just another vendor begging for money …"
- "You're going to think I don't understand how hard it is to juggle your cash …"
- "You're going to think I'm being a jerk …"

Then, I delivered my "I" Message: "When you continually fail to live up to your financial obligations to me, I feel concerned because I'm not sure how I can continue to provide my services if I'm wondering when I'll get paid."

This told him he was at risk of losing the partnership, without me having to say so outright. He promised to pay his outstanding invoice by the end of the day, and there haven't been any late payments since.

A Premature "I" Message

As one of the most experienced EOS Implementers (EOSIs), I sometimes train other EOSIs. In these group training sessions, there are varying degrees of expertise in the room. Beginners sometimes get frustrated because they're not having success yet, and they whine or try to place blame for it.

In one of these sessions, a relatively new EOSI went on the attack, saying the skills I was teaching weren't useful and I wasn't teaching what she really needed to know. At the time, I didn't know the motivation behind this; I didn't find out until later that she was struggling to sell her services and establish herself as an EOSI. I was conscious of the fact that

I had a lot of power in the room, and I didn't want to come off as a bully. However, I also felt pressured to stay on track with the schedule for the day and not let this person hold back the whole group.

So, I used an "I" Message: "When you continually interrupt us, I feel frustrated because it's slowing the whole group down."

There were several problems with this. First of all, it was too soon; I should have waited for the behavior to be repeated at least three times. Second, the "because" was not focused on what she stood to lose but on what others stood to lose. Third, I said it in front of the rest of the group, probably in an Assertive Tone.

The result was an "I" Message that was more like a weapon than a boundary, and it did *not* go over well. She disengaged completely from the session after that, and she resented me for calling her out that way for over a year. We eventually talked it out and repaired the relationship, but it was a mistake I'm always careful not to repeat.

Fifty Percent Discount

The Black Swan Team sometimes gets emails from readers of *Never Split the Difference* who simply want to share their stories about the power of Tactical Empathy. One person wrote to us admitting that when he first read the book, he thought it was entertaining but probably not very practical. Shortly afterward, he found himself in the buyer's seat in a negotiation. He didn't like the price and was ready to walk away if the seller wouldn't come down.

On a whim, he decided to try one thing he remembered from the book: "How am I supposed to do that?" With that one question, the seller offered him a 50 percent discount, as well as a month-to-month contract instead of a long-term agreement. "I felt like I was using the Force," the reader told us. Until you test the boundaries, you never know how far your counterpart might go to keep you at the table.

Walkaway Power

Recently, I used the Phases of No to great effect with an aggressive salesperson who wasn't listening to me. The conversation started because I had some existing content that EOS wanted to republish as a video course—the first in a series of many courses they planned to make. So, the leader of the project, Darren, put me in touch with a video course company that could create and distribute the product.

Before I got on the call, it was my understanding that Darren had made a special arrangement with the video course company. However, as soon as the salesperson started talking, it was clear that he was treating me like any retail customer, just giving me his canned spiel. I said, "*How am I supposed to do that*, when Darren told me the terms of the deal were one thing and now you're telling me something else?"

He placated me, saying maybe they could do a deal where the cost was covered by royalties on the back end. I said that was fine with me, but then he didn't follow through on it. After the conversation, he sent an email that was clearly the same follow-up he sends to every client, with the standard terms and even a rah-rah video about the benefits of partnering with his company.

I replied:

> It seems like you're avoiding the question of how we structure the deal. I asked a simple question. I got another sales pitch asking me to watch videos, puffing about abundance. *This is not going to work for me.*
>
> Best of luck.

I really was willing to walk away. The project would have benefited me, but not so much that I was willing to invest significant money in it or waste time negotiating with someone who wasn't even listening. And by walking away, I found out that the salesperson was not so set on his standard terms. He went back to Darren and ironed out the deal properly. Now, the project is moving forward, with EOS covering the costs instead of me.

IN SHORT ...

- An "I" Message is a technique for confronting persistent counterproductive behavior without sounding accusatory.
    - It has a specific structure: "When you _____, I feel _____ because _____."
    - The "because" part of the statement should focus on what your counterpart has to lose if they don't change their behavior.
    - Set up an "I" Message with an Accusations Audit, and follow it with Dynamic Silence.
    - Use it only after a bad behavior has been repeated at least three times.
    - Be very careful not to weaponize it. This is a very assertive move, and if not delivered properly, it can easily backfire.
    - When you need to hold your ground in a negotiation, use the Four Phases of No.
- These phrases convey that you're willing to walk away without explicitly threatening to walk away.
    - Your delivery—especially your tone of voice—is key to successfully being assertive without offending your counterpart.

LOW-STAKES PRACTICE

To start getting comfortable with these assertive tools, do these exercises.

1. **Use an "I" Message to address low-stakes counterproductive behavior.** For example, try it with a friend or relative who has a habit of interrupting you, with a client who has a propensity for "scope creep," or with a colleague who routinely shows up five minutes late. Remember the structure: "When you _____, I feel _____ because _____."
2. **Practice saying no without saying, "No."** When you need to say no to a low-stakes request, try using the Phases of No instead. This conveys that you're willing to walk away without offending your counterpart. Remember the sequence: "How am I supposed to do that?" ➜ "That just doesn't work for me." ➜ "I can't do that." ➜ "No."

To learn more about "I" Messages, scan the QR code and join the Black Swan Community.

PART IV

THE NEXT LEVEL

Congratulations! If you've read all the way to this point, you've gotten a thorough introduction to the most important and commonly used Black Swan skills. The fun isn't over yet, though. The next four chapters will take you to the next level with concepts and tools that build on the fundamentals you've already studied. Here's what you're about to learn:

- How to adjust your communication style for different kinds of people
- How to find out fast whether your counterpart really intends to work with you
- How to make sure your agreements actually get implemented
- How to ask questions that are more likely to get the answer you want

CHAPTER 15

NEGOTIATOR PERSONALITY TYPES

Everything you've learned so far—all the Black Swan skills—works well with all kinds of people. No matter who they are, where they're from, or what they do, every human being has a deep-seated need to feel understood by someone else. That's exactly what the Black Swan skills are designed to achieve, so they're effective universally.

That said, people are not all the same. They will not all respond exactly the same way to the things you say and do, especially when they're under pressure or feeling triggered. That's OK—remember, Tactical Empathy is improv, not a scripted play. You're not following a formula; you're responding in real time to what's in front of you, with the tools at your disposal. The better you understand what's in front of you—or more accurately, *who* is in front of you—the easier it will be to choose an effective response.

That's what the Negotiator Personality Types are for. When we look at the broad patterns of how people think and behave in sensitive conversations, we find they fall into three categories. You're already familiar with these categories from our discussion of Tone in chapter 11: Assertive, Analyst, and Accommodator.*

These categories are not intended to capture who you are on any given Tuesday. Rather, they describe your instinctive tendencies when you're *under pressure.* When your back is against the wall and you just got punched in the face, what do you do? When you're feeling threatened and don't have the time or presence of mind to think things through, what's your default response? That's what the Negotiator Personality Types are about—not how you act when everything is puppies and rainbows, but how you act when you're under attack.

Let's be crystal clear up front: None of the three types is better than any other. Each one brings value to the table, and each one has weaknesses. The important thing to understand is that each type has slightly different perspectives on the factors at play in a sensitive conversation—factors like time, silence, conflict, and compromise. When you're blind to the Negotiator Personality Types involved in a conversation, invisible misalignments over those things can derail the dialogue. Understanding your own type and that of your counterpart helps you avoid those problems and adjust your style to communicate more effectively.

In this chapter, you'll take the assessment that identifies your Negotiator Personality Type. Then we'll explore each of the three types in detail, as well as the problems to watch out for with each combination of personalities in a sensitive conversation.

THE NEGOTIATOR PERSONALITY TYPE ASSESSMENT

Before you answer these eighteen questions, a reminder: There are no right or wrong answers. Each type has its good side and its bad side.

---

* These are loosely based on the Thomas–Kilmann Conflict Modes. However, we've modified that framework to better fit what we've observed in the real world from decades of conducting and teaching high-stakes negotiation.

Forget about what you wish you were or what you think we would want you to be and just respond truthfully. The right answer is the *honest* answer.

For each of the following questions, pick the response that sounds *most* like you. Don't skip any questions.

1. Focus—How do I focus my thinking during the negotiation process?
   a. I prefer to focus on the things that we agree on.
   b. I prefer to focus on thinking everything through thoroughly.
   c. I prefer to be focused on my goals.

2. Tension—How do I deal with tension during sensitive conversations?
   a. It's more important to soothe others' feelings and relieve tension before finding a solution.
   b. Tension is useless.
   c. Tension can be very productive.

3. Relationship—How do I see the value of relationships?
   a. Our relationship must be protected.
   b. Relationships are not particularly relevant.
   c. Relationships are incidental.

4. Apologies—How do I feel about giving and receiving apologies?
   a. If offense has been taken, an apology is a necessity before a productive relationship can continue.
   b. Apologies aren't relevant to the analysis of the data.
   c. Apologies are a cheap currency. Don't be so thin-skinned.

5. Reciprocity—How do I feel about giving and receiving gifts or concessions?
   a. I am the first to give, and I will always give in return.
   b. Gifts are often a trap.
   c. My gains were earned and logical. I may owe something in return occasionally, but I need to have a good reason for it.

6. Time—How do I think about the effective use of my time?
   a. Time spent building the relationship is time well spent.
   b. Haste makes waste.
   c. Time is money.

7. Conflict—How do I view the role of conflict in negotiation?
   a. If it makes others happy, I will agree to their perspective.
   b. Conflict is counterproductive.
   c. Conflict is part of the game.

8. Silence—How do I assess the value/impact of silence during sensitive conversations?
   a. Silence = anger.
   b. Silence is an opportunity to think.
   c. Silence is an opportunity to push ahead.

9. Relationship—How important to me is being "liked" by my counterpart?
   a. Being liked is the most important thing.
   b. Being liked has no relevance to the effectiveness of our deal.
   c. Being liked is useful if it helps me get my way.

10. Compromise—How do I view compromise during negotiations?
    a. Compromise is a great idea as long as they feel it's fair.
    b. Compromise is a poor solution.
    c. I hate compromise.

11. Perspective—How do I view sharing my opinion/perspective?
    a. It's better to preserve the relationship than to share something that will hurt someone's feelings.
    b. I am careful about revealing too much.
    c. I drive to get my points across.

12. Fairness—How do I view the concept of fairness in negotiation?
    a. The deal must be fair to all sides.
    b. "Fair" is too subjective to even be considered a factor.
    c. All's fair in love and war. Negotiation is a battle.

13. BATNA—How important to me is knowing the Best Alternative to a Negotiated Agreement?
    a. I have to know my options so I don't get pushed past them.
    b. My alternatives are simply other possibilities, nothing more.
    c. Best alternative? Ha! I'm here to win.

14. Preparation—What is the process to prepare for a negotiation?
    a. I need to get to know my counterpart so we can connect as people.

b. I need to have all the data possible available to me that may affect the outcomes.
   c. The goal is clear. I know what I want. That's all the preparation I need.

15. Feelings—How do I see the role of feelings in negotiations?
    a. It matters to me how they feel about the deal.
    b. Feelings and emotions are impediments to dispassionate analysis.
    c. Feelings? Seriously? Get over it.

16. Anger—How do I view the use of anger in sensitive conversations?
    a. I hate it. I feel guilty when I feel it. They must apologize if they use it before we can continue.
    b. It obstructs thinking. If they use it, they will always be that way. I will withdraw and avoid engaging again.
    c. It works! I may be able to use it to get my way. If they get angry with me, no big deal. Negotiation can be combat anyway. Get over it.

17. Honesty—How important to me is telling the truth in a negotiation?
    a. If a problem or an issue will offend or cause problems, I will protect the relationship first and say something to keep things running smoothly in the hopes the problem will self-correct.
    b. If they are not smart enough to find it out themselves, I'm not responsible for doing their work for them.
    c. I am nothing if not honest. If it comes out of my mouth, it's the truth. Deal with it.

18. Mistakes—What is my perspective on mistakes made in the deal or the negotiation?
    a. Let's not talk about it, especially if it will cause problems. Things will work out.
    b. Mistakes are due to a lack of analysis and preparation. They are embarrassing and have to be avoided.
    c. What's the big deal? Fix it and move on. Time is money, and I hate indecision.

Now that you've answered all eighteen questions, add up how many As, Bs, and Cs you got. You will almost certainly have a mix, but one category should stand out as significantly more than the rest. If you got mostly As, you're an Accommodator. Mostly Bs means you're an Analyst. Mostly Cs, you're an Assertive. (More on what those mean in a moment.)

You might be wondering: What if I'm a little of all three? Is that possible? To put it bluntly, no. You can certainly be a little of all three when things are going well, but when the pressure is on, you will default to just *one* of the types.

Think of it this way: If you're hiking in the woods and a bear comes out of nowhere and is about to attack, what do you do? The Assertive pulls out a knife and goes *mano a mano*—even if he doesn't make it, that bear will know who he was messing with. The Analyst pulls out a map and finds the nearest escape route; he planned for this possibility ahead of time. The Accommodator tries to calm the bear down and give it some food; he knows that bear just needs a little love.

If no single category stands out as the strongest in your assessment results, you were probably thinking too hard about your answers or not keeping the right context in mind. Who are you when the enemy is inside the wire and you're passing out the last of the ammunition? If you're still not sure, just keep reading. Once you get a clearer picture of each type, it will be easier to know which one fits you best.

We've done this assessment at our live training events hundreds of times, and on average, the room usually breaks out into thirds. That means every time you go into a sensitive conversation, there's a two-thirds chance the other person has a different Negotiator Personality Type (and by extension, worldview) than you do. If you don't figure out who they really are, there's a good chance you'll inadvertently do something to alienate them. So, let's dig into the three types and find out what makes each one tick.

THE ASSERTIVE

Primary motivation: Being heard and respected

What an Assertive cares about above all else—even above getting what they want in the deal—is respect. We've said before that all human beings want to be understood by someone else, and that's true, but for an Assertive, it's priority number one. Until they feel that you hear and respect their position, you won't get anywhere with them. So, focus first on what they have to say; they'll only listen to you if they're convinced you understand them.

Afraid of: Losing respect and dignity

The flip side of their motivation is their fear; they want to avoid feeling disrespected at all costs. They would rather blow up the deal and walk away empty-handed than tolerate a perceived lack of respect. Because of that, it's extremely important to be deferential toward an Assertive and take care to avoid slighting them.

How they see themselves: Honest, logical, and direct

Assertives love to get right to the point in all their interactions. They say what they mean, and they mean what they say. They will not mince words or beat around the bush; they would rather tell it like they see it and let the chips fall where they may. They take pride in their direct, clear way of communicating because (in their view) it saves time and avoids confusion.

How others might see them: Emotional, aggressive, and harsh

Because Assertives don't soften their words, other people often perceive them as aggressive. When Assertives feel strongly about something and want to be clear about it, they have a tendency to raise their voices; they're the type of people who will yell, "I'm not yelling!" This tone typically doesn't offend other Assertives, who can have a shouting match with someone and then shake hands and be fine. However, it doesn't fly with the other two personality types. Analysts will view it as counterproductive, and Accommodators will think they offended the Assertive. Both tend to withdraw as a result.

View of business relationships: They need respect—nothing more or less

Assertives do not walk into a negotiation hoping to make friends. They don't care if you like them, and they don't need to like you. They only care about whether you respect them. As long as there is respect, they're happy to do business.

Time = Money

Assertives are not patient people. To them, time is money, so they *hate* to waste it, and they feel deeply disrespected when they think their counterpart is dragging their feet, stalling, or being indecisive. They want to find out as quickly as possible whether they're going to be able to get what they want out of an interaction. Their nightmare scenario is spending a long time on a negotiation that doesn't pan out in the end.

Silence = An opportunity to talk more

Assertives love to hold the floor. Because their number one priority is being heard and respected, they take every opportunity to say what's on their minds. They will not tolerate silence for long—not because it makes them uncomfortable but because they want you to hear them.

Implementation: They'll figure it out later

Assertives are far more concerned with beating you into a "yes" than figuring out how the agreement will be implemented. They may rush into an agreement only to find out later that they can't execute as promised. This means you should test any agreement with an Assertive at least twice using Calibrated Questions.

Reciprocity: They give only what they have to and take everything they can get

Assertives enter every negotiation hoping to give up as little as possible and get as much as possible. They don't make concessions easily, and when they do, they're counting the seconds until they get something of equal or more value. By the same token, every concession they receive from the other side is a win, and they have no qualms about pushing to get as much as they can.

Compromise: They don't like to do it

Because they take pride in getting the most and giving up the least, compromise feels like a loss to them.

BATNA (Best Alternative to a Negotiated Agreement): There isn't one

For an Assertive, anything other than getting what they want is a loss. They hate to lose and they never plan on losing, so they typically don't think in advance about what they will do if they don't get to a negotiated agreement.

How to get them back: Any invitation to reengage

Of the three personality types, Assertives are the easiest to bring back to the table if you've inadvertently driven them away. You don't need to grovel or soothe their hurt feelings. Just extend an invitation to reengage that affirms your respect for them and your serious intentions to come to an agreement.

Worst type match: Analyst

(You'll see why later in this chapter.)

What's good about negotiating with Assertives

They're highly logical. A strong rational argument will often sway them.

They're straightforward. You don't have to worry about whether they meant what they said.

They're goal oriented. Perfecting the solution is less important than getting it done.

They're hard to offend. As long as they feel heard and respected, you won't drive them away. They view negotiations as intellectual sparring and enjoy doing battle. To them, conflict isn't personal—it's just business.

What to watch out for with Assertives

They love winning above all else. You'll have more success if you can find a way to get what you want while letting them feel like they're winning.

You might get triggered. As we mentioned before, they tend to have an aggressive communication style (which they don't view as aggressive). Plus, they view negotiations as an opportunity to explain why they're right and you're wrong. It's easy to get offended, so be prepared for it.

They're prone to tunnel vision. If they get too focused on just one goal or solution, they'll miss opportunities to explore other options.

They're highly emotional. Strong emotions—especially negative ones—can cloud their decision-making.

They're prone to happy ears. When they get a yes, they believe it's a done deal because they assume other people also say what they mean. In reality, their counterpart often hasn't fully committed yet.

They tend to neglect implementation. They want the win in the moment; they'll worry about the how later. That can lead to deals falling apart after an apparent agreement has been reached.

They're prone to information overload. They have little patience for lots of data because they feel it bogs them down and impedes the progress of the conversation.

THE ANALYST

Primary motivation: Acquiring information

What Analysts care about most, even more than getting what they want in the deal, is getting smarter. They want to validate the information they have and add to their body of knowledge. If they can do that, they'll be OK even if they don't come to an agreement in the negotiation.

Afraid of: Being wrong

The last thing an Analyst wants is to make a bad decision because they didn't have the full picture. To them, a mistake isn't just a mistake; it's a reflection of their self-worth and identity. Because of this, they'll take extra care to make sure their information is complete and accurate, and they've taken every important factor into account.

How they see themselves: Realistic, prepared, and smart

Analysts take pride not just in getting things done but in getting them exactly right. They are optimizers and perfectionists; good enough is not good enough for them. At the same time, they are pragmatic, not idealistic; they want to nail down exactly how something is going to happen before they agree to it. To them, anything else is a waste of time and a disservice to everyone involved.

How others might see them: Cold, aloof, and hard to read

Because Analysts are so focused on the facts and because they're reluctant to say anything they're not one hundred percent sure of, they can come off as unfriendly or aloof. Assertives typically view them as reticent and hard to read, which frustrates the Assertives because they value straightforwardness. Accommodators tend to find Analysts hard to connect with, which frustrates the Accommodators because they value personal relationships.

View of business relationships: As long as they aren't causing conflict, they are actively preserving the relationship

Analysts don't think of business relationships as something they need to nurture. In their view, all they need to do is avoid causing offense. They don't need to get to know the other person or feed their ego to have a successful business relationship.

Time = Preparation

Analysts do not love to think or make decisions on their feet. They like to take their time and have all the information in front of them so they can avoid making a mistake. They value having time before, during, and after a conversation to think things through carefully, without being rushed.

Silence = Time to think

Remember the story we told in chapter 8 about the televised interview where Elon Musk sat in silence for twenty-two seconds before answering a question? That's what Analysts will do with silence. They appreciate having that space to think, so give it to them and don't interrupt their thought process.

Implementation: It's a prerequisite for any agreement

For the Analysts, "yes" is nothing without the "how." Before they commit to anything, they want to be completely clear on how it will be executed. They don't want to make any promises they can't keep, and they don't want the other side to disappoint them down the line.

Reciprocity: They think hard before giving and are suspicious of unsolicited gifts

Analysts do not make concessions on a whim. They only give up things they've already thought long and hard about, which means they feel confident that it's a concession worth making. Because of this, they're suspicious of receiving anything unsolicited from the other side; they assume it must be a trap.

Compromise: They're willing to use it as a strategic move

For an Analyst, any concession—including a compromise—is a calculated move. If they've done the analysis and determined it's worth compromising to get what they really care about, they'll have no problem doing it.

BATNA: It's just another option

Analysts like to think through every possible consideration and have a contingency plan for everything. If a negotiated agreement isn't possible, the BATNA is simply another possible course of action—another move to play if it becomes necessary.

How to get them back:
Show them you're ready to get something accomplished

If an Analyst walks away from the table, it's usually because (a) they think you haven't adequately prepared for the negotiation, (b) your data is faulty, or (c) they feel pressured to make decisions they're not ready to make. You won't win them back with just an apology—apologies have little value to Analysts. Instead you need to show that you're ready to work with them by acknowledging the work they put into preparing for the negotiations and the validity of the information they brought to the table.

Worst type match: Assertive

(More on this in a moment.)

What's good about negotiating with Analysts

They're highly prepared. They will do their research and planning ahead of time so they're ready to go when you actually get in the room with them.

They're methodical and diligent. They will make sure every relevant factor has been taken into consideration, and all the i's are dotted and t's are crossed.

They're focused on implementation. They want to make sure that what you've agreed on actually happens, so they'll insist on working out the kinks before everyone walks away.

What to watch out for with Analysts

Lack of preparation offends them. If you come into the negotiation unprepared, it conveys the message that you're not taking it as seriously as they are.

They need time to think. They are slow to answer calibrated questions, so be patient and give them plenty of Dynamic Silence.

They need time to decide. Don't expect an agreement on the first interaction. Sometimes, they may appear to agree to something when they're really just agreeing to think about it.

They hate surprises. They need time to process new information, so give it to them in advance if possible, or give them plenty of time to digest it before asking them to make any decisions about it.

They dislike heated discussion. They view emotional outbursts and raised voices as counterproductive, and they would rather withdraw from the conversation than engage with that kind of behavior.

They're skeptical by nature. They want to see evidence, so bring data to back up your claims.

They prefer to work alone. They're very autonomous and would often rather go away and think things through on their own than figure it out collaboratively in the moment.

THE ACCOMMODATOR

Primary motivation: Building the relationship

Accommodators care about relationships above all else. Even if an agreement doesn't get reached or they don't get everything they wanted, they're happy as long as the relationship is strong.

Afraid of: Damaging the relationship

The flip side of this is that they hate to see a relationship go bad. The last thing they want is to offend anyone, drive them away, or fail to make a connection.

How they see themselves:
Personable, conversational, and caring

Because Accommodators value relationships so highly, they place extreme importance on being good at connecting with others. They take pride in being skilled at putting others at ease and keeping the conversation flowing. They think of themselves as good at listening, reading nonverbal signals, and building rapport. They also value knowing people on a personal level and taking an interest in them beyond the negotiation at hand.

How others might see them:
Overly friendly, talkative, and easy prey

Accommodators are usually seen as likable, but the other two personality types can become impatient with their chattiness. Assertives and Analysts like to get down to business, and Accommodators' preference for making personal connections first can be frustrating. Their desire to get to know their counterpart on a personal level can also feel intrusive to some.

View of business relationships:
Relationships are paramount and must be actively nurtured.

Accommodators take a proactive, hands-on approach to building rapport. They believe it's necessary to invest time in getting to know their counterpart and to build goodwill by demonstrating a willingness to collaborate.

Time = Relationship building

For Accommodators, building relationships is time well spent.

Silence = Upsetting, indicates anger

Because Accommodators believe it's important to keep the conversation flowing, they strongly dislike silence. They tend to assume it means they've done something wrong—that they've offended, confused, or upset their counterpart in some way. Their instinct is to break the silence either by explaining themselves further or by asking a question.

Implementation: Every yes is conditional

Accommodators *hate* to disappoint people. They'll tell you almost anything to keep from disappointing you, even if they know they can't follow through on it. In most cases, a yes is at best a maybe, more likely a no. They're not going to push for clarity on implementation, and they're very likely to overpromise. That means you need to test any agreement with multiple Calibrated Questions (even more than with Assertives).

Reciprocity: They give proactively to build goodwill, and they view gifts from others as confirmation of a positive relationship

Accommodators are the most likely to give something up first. Their giving isn't motivated by an expectation of reciprocity but by a desire to build the relationship. When their counterpart makes a concession, they tend to view it as flattering—a sign of positive regard by the other person.

Compromise: They believe it's necessary in order to maintain a relationship

Accommodators are the most comfortable with compromise out of the three types. They see compromise, like giving, as a move that builds goodwill. So, they're willing to do it, often even if it means sacrificing something they want.

BATNA: Permission to stand their ground

For an Accommodator, having an alternative to a negotiated agreement allows them to draw a clear line in the sand. If their counterpart steps over it, they don't have to play nice anymore, because they have a plan B if the relationship blows up. Without this, they're prone to overconceding and getting trampled.

How to get them back: Apologize sincerely

If you've caused a rift with an Accommodator, any attempt to reengage *must* begin with a sincere, heartfelt apology. They need to see that you recognize the hurt you've caused and that you value the relationship enough to repair it. Do not attempt to get back to business before investing time in acknowledging how they feel and understanding how to make it right.

Worst type match: Accommodator

(More on this shortly.)

What's good about negotiating with Accommodators

They're happy when communicating. They love to talk and are generally willing to share information. Because they often take the conversation beyond the bounds of the issue at hand (in an effort to build the relationship), they may reveal black swans that help you understand their circumstances and motivations.

They're good listeners. They are tuned in to both verbal and nonverbal signals, and they're naturally good at making others feel heard.

They're optimistic. They tend to enter a conversation believing the problems at hand are solvable. They want to believe the best of people and will give them the benefit of the doubt over minor offenses.

They love to help. They prefer collaboration to confrontation, and they get great satisfaction from solving other people's problems. If they can get what they need while giving you what you want, they consider that a win.

What to watch out for with Accommodators

They will overpromise. They hate to disappoint others, so they often say yes to things they won't actually follow through on. Any concession you get from an Accommodator must be tested repeatedly to increase the likelihood of implementation. Pay close attention to their tone and body language; they might not express hesitancy in words, but it will show.

They're poor time managers. Because they love to spend time building relationships, they easily get distracted from the issue at hand and lose track of time.

They hate confrontation. They are peace-seekers, and they are highly sensitive to tone, so heated conflict is extremely uncomfortable for them. They will do almost anything to avoid it, including making promises they can't keep.

Reciprocity means a lot to them. Yes, they often give first without expecting quid pro quo. However, if they never receive anything in return, they take that as an indication that their counterpart doesn't value the relationship.

Long fuse, big explosion. Because they're optimistic and hate confrontation, Accommodators will tolerate a lot of bad behavior from their counterparts. However, as soon as they realize the relationship isn't as important to the other person as it is to them, it's over. Once they've been offended to that degree, there's no going back—no chance of repairing the relationship or making a deal. As Derek likes to say, you'd have a better chance of scratching a bobcat behind the ears in a phone booth.

WORST TYPE MATCHES AND OTHER PITFALLS

As you can see, there are some fundamental differences in values, beliefs, and behaviors among the three personality types. These differences can lead to serious missteps and misunderstandings in a sensitive conversation and possibly blow it up completely. But fortunately, such misalignments are predictable and easy to prevent if you know your own type and can make an educated guess about your counterpart. Let's look at the most common issues that come up and how to forestall them.

Worst Type Match: Assertive and Analyst

Assertives and Analysts clash big-time on three key dimensions: time, silence, and implementation.

For Assertives, time is money, and they want to bang out an agreement as quickly as possible. Analysts hate to rush because they want to be thorough and think through all the details before they come to an agreement. Assertives feel like Analysts are dragging their feet and wasting time; Analysts feel like Assertives are pushing them to make rash decisions.

When it comes to silence, Assertives want to fill it; they'll take the floor every chance they get because they want to be heard. Analysts use the silence as time to process, and breaking it derails their train of thought. So, Assertives get impatient at Analysts who don't answer quickly enough, and Analysts get frustrated at Assertives who never give them space to think.

On implementation, Assertives want the "yes" in the moment; they'll worry about "how" down the road. This drives Analysts absolutely crazy because they view a "yes" without a "how" as worthless.

Fortunately, the solutions to these misalignments are simple, as long as you're aware of the personalities at play.

If you're an Analyst and your counterpart is an Assertive, you should expect them to move at a faster pace than you do. Know that when they push to move forward, they're not trying to undermine your thought process; they just don't realize that you need more time. You need to ask for more time directly, explain why you need it, and tell them exactly when you'll have an answer for them. As long as they're convinced it will move the conversation forward in a productive way, they will give you the time you need.

The same is true when it comes to silence. Remember that your Assertive counterpart doesn't know you need the silence to think. To them, it's an irresistible temptation to talk more. So when you need more silence, you have to ask for it directly. They want to get to an agreement as fast as possible; if you let them know that giving you space to think will move the discussion forward more quickly, they will be happy to give it to you.

Let's flip this around and say you're the Assertive and your counterpart is an Analyst. You're going to feel like your counterpart is dragging things out, but they're not trying to waste your time. They're only trying to make sure they do things right and come to an agreement they can actually follow through on. It's in your best interests to give them the time and silence they need to think. Rushing them will undermine your rapport and increase their hesitation to commit; instead, seek to increase their confidence by validating their information and analysis.

Worst Type Match: Accommodator and Accommodator

Accommodators are pretty good at handling their misalignments with Assertives and Analysts; they're willing to adapt to their counterpart's style. Put two Accommodators together, and they will have a great time … and get nothing accomplished. They tend to be so focused on building the relationship that they're reluctant to get down to business, and each side will hesitate to say anything that the other side might not like.

If you and your counterpart are both Accommodators, keep this tendency in mind. The relationship matters, but at some point, you need to address the issue at hand. Know that your counterpart (just like you) is prone to saying things they don't mean just to keep you happy. So when you're trying to understand their perspective, use creative Labels and Mislabels to make sure you're getting the full story. When you're crafting an agreement, use plenty of Calibrated Questions to nail down exactly how the agreement will be implemented. In general, take every "yes" with a grain of salt and test it thoroughly to make sure it's real.

Other Risks: Assertives and Accommodators

The dangerous misalignment with Assertives and Accommodators has to do with reciprocity and compromise. Assertives want to give as little and take as much as possible, and they hate to compromise. Accommodators will give freely to build goodwill, and they view compromise as a necessary part of a healthy relationship. That's a recipe for a one-sided dynamic, where the Accommodator gives and gives, and the Assertive takes and takes. When an Assertive receives an unsolicited concession, they aren't thinking about how they should reciprocate; they're wondering how much more they can get. And they might get a lot … until they go too far and the Accommodator starts to think they don't care about the relationship. Once that line is crossed, there's no saving the relationship or the negotiation.

If you're an Accommodator and your counterpart is an Assertive, keep in mind that they don't view giving the same way you do. You want to give them something to sow goodwill, but they won't see it that way; they'll see it as an invitation to take advantage of you. In fact, Assertives don't appreciate gifts the way you do. They place more value on something they had to fight for than something that was given to them freely. Instead of using concessions to build goodwill, focus on making them feel heard and respected, which is what they really want.

If you're an Assertive and your counterpart is an Accommodator, rein in your instinct to take a mile when they give an inch. When it comes to reciprocity, you don't know exactly where their line in the sand is and you don't want to risk crossing it. If you do—if you take too much without giving enough in return—you risk driving them away. Once an Accommodator is gone, they just might be gone for good, so don't push your luck. Be sure to make at least occasional concessions to reassure them that you appreciate them and value the relationship.

Other Risks: Analysts and Accommodators

Analysts and Accommodators generally work pretty well together, but there can be friction in a couple of areas. One is around reciprocity: Accommodators give first to build goodwill, but Analysts see an unsolicited concession as a potential trap. Instead of strengthening the relationship as the Accommodator intended, the move actually puts the Analysts in a defensive mode. The other misalignment is around how time is spent: Accommodators want to get to know their counterparts, and Analysts want to focus on thinking through the issue at hand. Each one can get frustrated with the other for focusing on the "wrong" thing.

If you're an Accommodator and your counterpart is an Analyst, keep these tendencies in mind. Know that giving them something they haven't asked for might actually be counterproductive, leading them to mistrust rather than appreciate you. Also know that while *you* want to get to know each other first and get to business later, *they* want to do the opposite. If you insist on trying to make a personal connection before you've discussed the main issue at hand, you'll be met with resistance. You'll have much more success if you wait until afterward.

The opposite applies if you're an Analyst and your counterpart is an Accommodator. Recognize that an unsolicited gift from an Accommodator is just what it seems: a gift. Show your appreciation and reciprocate if you can, even if it's in a small way. They will probably try to make small talk at the beginning of the conversation. Don't try to change the subject right away; be receptive to their efforts to make a connection, at least for a few minutes. Once they see that you care about the relationship, it will be easier to direct their attention to the real purpose of the conversation.

A Note on Apologies

People underestimate the power of a sincere apology. Although not everyone values apologies equally, if you sense that your counterpart is offended or hurt, an apology is a good place to start. That said, an effective apology is more than just "I'm sorry." It also needs to recognize what the offense was, acknowledge the impact it made, and give your counterpart an opportunity to fully express their feelings on the matter.

Here's a good way to phrase it: "I'm sorry, it's clear that I did or said something to offend you. Would you be opposed to walking me through exactly where that offense started?"

Even if you know what you did, this gives them a chance to vent, which allows their negative emotions to come down and their rational thinking to go up. That gives you a much better chance of moving forward in a productive way.

IN SHORT ...

- There are three Negotiator Personality Types: Assertive, Analyst, and Accommodator.
- *Assertives* care most about being heard and respected.
- *Analysts* care most about gathering information.
- *Accommodators* care most about building relationships.
- When you're under pressure and can't think clearly, you will default to *one* of these three patterns of beliefs and behaviors.
- These personality types operate on different beliefs and assumptions, which can lead to misunderstandings and unintended offenses in sensitive conversations.
- If you know your type and can make an educated guess about your counterpart, you can adjust your behavior to avoid these problems.

Low-Stakes Practice

To start getting familiar with the Negotiator Personality Types, do these exercises.

1. **Cold read a room.** When you're in a social environment with multiple people you don't know well, gather data with your eyes. Observe their behavior and make educated guesses about their Negotiator Personality Types. Assertives are likely to be holding court, putting themselves at the center of attention; Accommodators are the social butterflies who try to connect with as many people as possible; Analysts will probably be hanging back, observing rather than initiating engagement.
2. **Assess someone you know well.** Focus on someone you know well, like a family member, a good friend, or a close colleague. Think about them as you read through the profiles in this chapter again. Which sounds most like them? What behavior have you observed that backs up your conclusion?
3. **Adjust your communication style.** With the person you assessed in the previous exercise, adjust your communication style to fit their Negotiator Personality Type. Pay special attention to preventing the conflicts and misunderstandings you learned about earlier in this chapter. If it feels uncomfortable to you, you're probably doing it right.

To learn more about Negotiator Personality Types, scan the QR code and join the Black Swan Community.

CHAPTER 16

PROOF OF LIFE

In hostage negotiation, proof of life is literal. Before you invest time and resources in negotiating, you need to prove that the hostage is still alive. If not, there's nothing to talk about.

We know that in business negotiations, nobody's life is on the line. However, this same principle applies in a figurative way: You don't want to waste time on a conversation if the other side has no intention of ever coming to an agreement. Or, as Chris puts it so eloquently, "It's not a sin to lose business—it's a sin to take a long time to lose business."

That's what The Black Swan Group's Proof of Life is all about: saving you from wasting your time. In that way, it's one of the most selfish things we teach. Your counterpart doesn't get much benefit from it, but you do. In fact, the time, effort, and stress you save by using Proof of Life can make the difference between thriving and burning out in business.

THE FAVORITE AND THE FOOL

Research on the buying process has repeatedly shown one thing: There's no such thing as a truly open mind. By the time a potential buyer reaches out to you about your product or service, they're already more than halfway through their decision-making process. They've done at least some research to figure out what their options are and what attributes they should pay attention to. On top of that, they have personal preferences and past experiences that shape their thinking. They're already forming an opinion about what they want to do.

So before you ever talk to them, you're already either the Favorite or the Fool. The Favorite is the option they genuinely want, and they'll choose it at least 80 percent of the time. The Fool is there for due diligence, because it would be irresponsible not to at least look around, do a little comparison, and see what they might learn. The Fool gets chosen less than 20 percent of the time—usually only if the Favorite insists on a deal-breaker or if the Fool offers such an outrageous deal that the buyer can't justify passing it up.

If you think you've never been the Fool, think again. In *The Challenger Sale*, Matthew Dixon and Brent Adamson describe an unscientific survey of B2B buyers that asked how often they engage with a vendor they have no intention of choosing. The overwhelming answer was at least 20 percent of the time. That's probably a massive underestimation; people want to believe they have good intentions and open minds, and they tend to under-report anything that might reflect badly on them, even when the survey is anonymous. The reality is probably more like 60 percent of the time.

If you're the Favorite, it's obviously worth your time to pursue the conversation. If you're the Fool, it's not. It's that simple.

We know, a 20 percent chance of getting the business isn't *zero*—and that's the problem. People love to cling to the small probability that even if they're the Fool, they'll be able to make the sale. But ask yourself: Do you really want to do business with someone who sees you as their second choice? In the words of Joe Polish, they'll be HALF clients: hard, annoying, lame, and frustrating. They don't trust, value, or respect you the way they would if you were the Favorite, so they're going to push your boundaries and squeeze you for all you're worth. They'll be hard to please, which means they're unlikely to stick around or refer other people to you. In short, these are nightmare clients.

Your responsibility to *yourself* is to find out whether you're the Favorite or the Fool so you don't waste time chasing business you're never going to get. Is this a legitimate opportunity, or is this buyer just doing their due diligence or hoping to score some free consulting?

HOW TO GET PROOF OF LIFE

That's why we created the Proof of Life process. Not only does it save you from wasting your time, but it also decreases the chances of pushback on your terms. It does this by leading your counterpart to speak your value proposition before you ever have to. This is powerful; they're the ones telling you how great you are, instead of the other way around. That makes it much harder for them to backpedal later and argue that you're not worth the terms you're asking for.

It starts with one question: "Why me?"

We told you back in chapter 12 that you almost never want to ask why in a sensitive conversation, with one exception. This is that exception. "Why" puts people in a defensive position, which is usually a bad thing. But in this case, what you're asking them to defend is *you*. In that way, putting them on the defense actually works in your favor.

Phrase the "Why me?" question in a way that makes sense for your context. For example:

- "There are a lot of other _____ out there to _____. Why would you ever consider using me as your trusted _____?"

- "Of all the people you know in this space, why me?"
- "Of all the negotiation training companies out there, why would you want training from a bunch of hostage negotiators?"

Follow this with Dynamic Silence and listen closely to their response. What you're looking for is a *robust* answer. The more specific detail they give you, the more likely it is that you're the Favorite. Responses with robust detail might sound like:

- "We understand there are a lot of other ___, but we've read your Google reviews and they are almost all five stars. We've spoken with several people who have done business with you, and they all rave about your quality of work and transparency. For us, it was a real no-brainer."
- "You don't look or act like the other people in this space. Those others are snake-oil salesmen. They're just trying to tell you what you want to hear. I could tell the first time we talked that you're a straight shooter who provides quality services at a reasonable price. If we can make this work, I see a long and prosperous relationship for us going forward."
- "Who better than hostage negotiators to take this type of training from? I read *Never Split the Difference* four times. The translation from law enforcement to business is easy to understand. Plus, you guys are going to give us stuff based on real-world experience, not some academic pursuits. If I can apply what you guys used to do to my line of work, everything gets better. I can't wait!"

As they respond, use your Black Swan skills (e.g., Mirror, Label, Summary) to draw out all their thoughts on the subject and make them feel understood. Aim to get a clear signal of emotional buy-in (e.g., "That's right," "Exactly," etc.).

If a response doesn't sound particularly robust at first, call that out: "It sounds like you have some reservations about working with me." Sometimes, after removing yourself as a threat and inviting them to express themselves further, a mediocre response can turn into a robust one.

However, be careful to avoid getting happy ears—that is, hearing what you want to hear and assuming it's a done deal. If you hear something like "We're thinking about working with you" and you assume you're the Favorite, that's happy ears. They said something that sounded like a yes, but in reality they gave no firm indication that you're the Favorite.

IF YOU'RE THE FAVORITE ...

If you got a robust response in the Proof of Life conversation, the next step is to get them to articulate their vision of your partnership. (We'll address what to do about a not-so-robust response in the next section.) Remember the Law of Negotiation Gravity #10: Vision drives decision. As humans, when we intend to do something, we imagine it in advance. We play out the details and think through the hows and what-ifs in a kind of mental movie.

The idea here is to get your counterpart to narrate that movie for you. To do that, use what we call the Vision Label: "It sounds like you have a vision for what a business relationship with us would look like going forward."

The word *vision* is crucial here. Don't replace it with anything else. This word is the key to eliciting that mental movie.

Your goal is to find out what their expectations, hopes, and concerns are. Even if they know nothing about how you operate, they should be able to tell you what they want to experience in collaborating with *you* specifically. Use Labels and Mirrors to keep them talking and get as much detail as possible. The more they say about the benefits they expect to get from working with you, the better; if they articulate your value proposition themselves, it will be much harder for them to deny it later.

When they've fully expressed themselves, Summarize their vision. Be sure to get a signal of emotional buy-in (e.g., "That's right.") before moving on with the conversation.

From their vision, you should also get an idea of how their imagination lines up with the reality of working with you. It's crucial to address any misalignments up front and find out whether any of your standards—the things you're not willing to compromise on—are deal-breakers for them. This might include your price point, your timeline, your process, or any other terms they would have to agree to in order to work with you.

This probably sounds crazy. Most people try to avoid bringing up anything that might scare a buyer away. However, doing this up front is a crucial part of saving your time. The last thing you want is to spend a long time hammering out an agreement only to find out at the end that a crucial element of your terms is a deal-breaker for them. That puts you in a terrible position—either you have to walk away from a deal you've invested a lot of time in or you have to compromise your standards to push the deal through.

Neither option is good for you. You might be the Favorite, but if they're not willing to work within your standards, you don't want their business. Remember, one of the benefits of Tactical Empathy is that it allows you to be assertive without being offensive. In this case, it helps you hold your ground and say no to people who want to break your boundaries.

Because presenting your standards is an assertive move, preface it with a short Accusations Audit. For example:

- "This may be a deal-breaker for you guys."
- "This is probably not what you want to hear."

- "You are going to think I am trying to chase you away."

Then, lay out your terms in a direct, clear way, without making any attempt to sugarcoat them.

- "My work hours are _____ to _____ . I don't accept or make calls after that time."
- "We are incredibly, incredibly expensive."
- "We do not advise on cases involving familial disagreements."

As always, let the skill land with Dynamic Silence. You've just given your counterpart some very important information that may have thrown off all their expectations and calculations. They need plenty of time to digest it and decide how to respond.

One of my favorite examples of presenting standards comes from a real estate agent who found a way to inject humor into the conversation. After getting a positive response from the Proof of Life question and the Vision Label, she says, "I have some bad news … there are ten reasons you won't want to work with me."

"Ten reasons?" the client typically asks in surprise.

"Actually, it's only four," she says.

The client sighs in relief, and she presents her standards in a completely relaxed, casual manner. She's at ease, the client is at ease, and it doesn't feel like a battle or a test.

ARE YOU THE FOOL?

Throughout the Proof of Life conversation, watch for High-Risk Indicators (i.e., signs that you're the Fool). Your counterpart may act as if they want to do business with you, but if they actually have other motivations or intentions, it will show … if you know what to look for.

Indicator #1: They cannot or will not answer your "Why me?" question.
If you ask "Why me?" and get resistance, deflection, or vagueness in response, it's a good sign that you might be the Fool. This might sound like:

"That's for you to tell me."

"Why not you?"

"I'm researching my options."

There are several possible reasons for this. Maybe they're not the final decision-maker, so they don't care. Maybe they want to assert their superiority. Maybe they're on a fact-finding mission, just kicking your tires.

Whatever the reason, they're going to try to get you to answer your own question. Don't get sucked into this. Once you're explaining your value proposition, you've drifted from Tactical Empathy mode into chasing mode—and that's the last place you want to be.

Indicator #2: They appear not to have a vision of what the partnership is going to look like, or the vision doesn't include you.
As with the "Why me?" question, the response to the "vision" Label is very telling. If they cannot articulate their vision, or they do articulate a vision but it does not include you specifically, they probably do not intend to work with you.

Indicator #3: They're focused almost solely on discussions about price or commission.
If they show impatience when you talk about anything else (e.g., their vision of how this process will play out), you might be the Fool. When someone seems bent on manipulating you over price, it's usually because they're comparing your price to that of someone else who is the Favorite. They're not interested in what else might differentiate you from the competition. They have a specific price in mind, and what you charge is not lining up with what they imagined.

Indicator #4: They're overly focused on the details of your implementation plan.
If they're extremely keen to know exactly what you plan to do step by step, they may be pumping you for information as part of their due diligence. They want to compare your process to someone else's or take it to someone else for them to use—probably someone who is willing to do it for less. They're testing to see if you'll give them free consulting.

Here's how to respond to this behavior. First, give them a short Accusations Audit: "You're going to think I'm being an obnoxious jerk ..."

Then, make your standards clear: "I would be happy to provide you with the detail you're looking for once we establish a formal relationship. I'm not in the business of providing free consulting."

Because nobody else would say this, it sends the message that you're different, which often sparks their curiosity and keeps them engaged.

Indicator #5: They limit relationship building with you.
If you're the Fool, they might insist on a very short initial meeting—just long enough to ask the questions they want to ask. This shows that they feel obligated to have the conversation with you but don't really want to, or that they think their time is more valuable than yours.

Indicator #6: They're reluctant to share information.
If it feels like pulling teeth to get them talking about their circumstances, goals, concerns, et cetera, that's a strong indication that they don't trust you and don't plan on moving forward with you. After all, if you're going to be working together, you need to know these things and it's in their best interests to inform you. So if they're reluctant to inform you, it probably means you're not the partner they have in mind.

Indicator #7: They use the term "win-win" or "fair" in the opening exchange.
Back in chapter 10, we talked about how people sometimes weaponize fairness in a negotiation. If the conversation is just getting started and

right off the bat they try to pull that move, watch out. It might be a sign that down the road, they'll accuse you of some perceived unfairness to back out of the negotiation.

Indicator #8: They act like a diva.
If they're going on at length about the value of what *they're* bringing to *you*, beware. They might imply—or say outright—that you would be a fool to turn your back on the opportunity to work with them. That sends the signal that they value their own contribution more than yours and will use that as a reason to squeeze, manipulate, or otherwise mistreat you in the future.

Indicator #9: They're playing the victim.
Watch out for anyone who reacts to your pricing, process, or terms with anger or sadness. That means they're unable or unwilling to work within those terms and they want to turn that into a problem for *you* to solve. They'll criticize you, openly compare you to others, and adopt a judgmental or disappointed stance—all to pressure you into caving to their desires.

EXITING GRACEFULLY

When it's clear that you're the Fool and your counterpart has no intention of actually coming to an agreement with you, it's time to exit gracefully. This may happen right at the beginning of the conversation if they respond aggressively to your Proof of Life question. It might happen later, after multiple subtle High-Risk Indicators add up. Either way, exiting gracefully is how you protect your time while still maintaining a positive relationship and keeping the door open to future collaboration, if they ever want it. Here's what a graceful exit might sound like:

"I'm sorry, it's clear that you're still shopping around, which is a shame because I was really looking forward to the possibility of us working together. If the planets line up again and this opportunity presents itself in the future, I would be more than happy to reengage. Best of luck on your search."

There are three parts here.

First, a brief apology. You haven't done anything wrong, but it sounds deferential, which is important because you don't want to leave them feeling insulted.

Second, a "you" statement that recognizes you're not the Favorite. "You're clearly still shopping around." "It seems like you have some other great alternatives." "It sounds like you want to take your time to think things over." There are many possible variations, but they all focus on your counterpart (not you) and openly acknowledge that they're not ready to come to an agreement with you.

Third, a sincere invitation to reconnect in the future. "If your other options don't work out, you know where to find me." "If you ever decide this is a good fit for you, don't hesitate to reach out." Again, you can choose whatever wording feels right as long as you make them feel welcome to come back anytime.

REAL-WORLD EXAMPLES

Prepping for Deal-Breakers

Our client—let's call them JPK—was a large company that leased cranes to developers for major construction projects. Because their business involved lending expensive assets over a long period of time, they checked the credit of all their prospective customers and they usually only did business with those who had investment-grade credit. This minimized the risk that they would end up not getting paid for a crane that was in use on a construction site.

However, in this case, they were interested in doing a deal with a developer—let's call them Acme—who didn't have great credit. Acme was looking for a partner who could help position them as best in class, and they had reached out because they recognized JPK as a global leader in the space. The opportunity had the potential to be extremely profitable, but JPK would be assuming substantial risk and wanted to mitigate that with higher pricing and a five-year commitment.

JPK knew those terms might be deal-breakers for Acme, so they were careful to use Proof of Life to find out how serious Acme was about doing a deal. Andy, the JPK representative, opened up the dialogue with a brief Summary and a few Accusations Audits before asking an excellent Proof of Life question: "Joe, as I was preparing for this meeting, a question kept returning to my mind … there are clearly other places you could have gone—why did you reach out to us to be your trusted crane provider?"

Joe, the Acme representative, paused for a second, looked down at his feet, and then responded, "That's a great question … umm … your track record speaks for itself. We know you guys have the equipment and expertise to help us build faster and keep our labor costs down. You're a leader not only in the States but elsewhere. Quite frankly, it would be stupid not to go with you."

That is what we call a robust response. Andy Labeled, Mirrored, and Paraphrased what he heard to shore up the responses. At the end of the conversation, when he laid out JPK's terms, Joe appeared uncomfortable. He squirmed in his seat and furrowed his brow before saying, "I don't see how we could ever pay that."

Then Andy said, "I'm sorry … you're going to think I'm not the sharpest knife in the drawer. A few minutes ago, you said our track record spoke for itself, that you knew we could help you build faster, and that you would be stupid not to go with us. Now, you're saying we're not worth it. Those two things don't line up. How is what I'm hearing wrong?"

After several long seconds, Joe said, "Fair point. I'm just not sure what the executives on my side are gonna say." Andy used a few Calibrated Questions and Labels to confirm that Joe was going to do his level best to convince the C-suite. It took almost a full month, but the deal closed in the end.

Happy Ears and Wasted Effort

Our client, Misti, was an outstanding financial advisor—one of the top in her area. She had the right mindset, always pursuing quality relationships. No one worked harder than her. By all accounts, she was the personification of best practices for a financial professional.

One day, she received a phone call from a high-net-worth prospect who asked if she would be willing to meet to see if they were a good fit for each other. Misti prepared for the meeting diligently, spending hours on her pitch deck. She confirmed the appointment in advance and showed up on time, ready to go.

The meeting went perfectly: The prospect listened intently, seemed very engaged, and asked very specific questions. His attention never faded during the hour-long presentation. Misti explained everything from her service offerings and fees to her track record and experience. The prospect kept nodding and smiling, saying things like "Sounds good" and "Can't wait to work with you." At the end, he thanked Misti profusely and said how impressed he was with her depth and breadth of knowledge. He told her, "You've given me so much to think about. Let me process everything, and I'll get back to you shortly."

Misti left the meeting feeling like she nailed it. She desperately wanted to onboard this lucrative client, and she knew she was the best person for the job. Given that the appointment went better than expected, it seemed like a sure thing. This was going to be fun, not to mention a huge payday.

A few days later the phone rang. The prospect said, "Thank you again for all the information you provided, but I've decided to work with someone else."

Misti hung up the phone in absolute disbelief. She had never felt so right and been so wrong. This made no sense. She had done everything perfectly from start to finish. She was the obvious choice. What could have possibly happened? Did she say something wrong? Did she totally misread the situation? Did she not explain her value well enough?

None of the above. Her mistake was that she didn't execute Proof of Life. She was so excited about the positive feedback from the prospect that she didn't check to see if his intentions were serious. By skipping Proof of Life, Misti effectively did the heavy lifting for another financial advisor, who is now going to take her work and provide it to the prospect at a reduced rate. All those hours of preparation and presentation were totally wasted.

IN SHORT ...

- By the time a buyer reaches out to you, you're either the Favorite or the Fool. There's no such thing as an open mind.
- It's your responsibility to yourself to find out which one you are as quickly as possible. It's not a sin to lose business; it's a sin to take a long time to lose business.
- To get Proof of Life, ask "Why me?" and pay close attention to how they respond.
- Present your standards up front to make sure they're willing to work on your terms.
- Watch out for the nine indicators that you might be the Fool. If it becomes clear that you are, exit gracefully.

LOW-STAKES PRACTICE

To start getting comfortable with Proof of Life, do these exercises.

1. **Practice your "Why me?" question.** If you're in a position where you talk to prospective clients, you'll ask this same question over and over. So, prepare it in advance—think about your typical sales situation and formulate the version of this question that makes the most sense for you. Practice it in the mirror at least 20 times; building some muscle memory with it will help you overcome any nerves when the time comes to use it with a prospect.
2. **Practice your Vision Label.** Same idea here. The Vision Label is some variation on "It sounds like you have a vision for what a business relationship with us would look like going forward." Tweak this to fit your context, but be sure to keep the word "vision." You will use this Label repeatedly, so prepare and practice it in advance.
3. **Practice stating your standards.** Make a list of your deal-breakers with clients—the terms, boundaries, or processes you're not willing to compromise. Practice these in the mirror or with a colleague, and refine your delivery until you feel fully comfortable saying these things out loud. It should feel a lot like an Accusations Audit, even if the sentences don't have that particular structure.

To learn more about Proof of Life, scan the QR code and join the Black Swan Community.

CHAPTER 17

THREE TYPES OF AGREEMENT

If you have kids—or if you remember being a kid—you know how hard it can be to get them to do what they promise to do.

"I need you to get your laundry done today," you tell them.

"OK," they say.

Are they going to do it? Yeah, right. That "OK" wasn't a real agreement. It was a "stop nagging me so I can get on with what I actually want to do" agreement. Or, in Tactical Empathy terms, a *counterfeit* agreement.

If you want to see clean, folded clothes in your kid's closet, you know you can't take that first agreement at face value. So you ask, "What does your day look like, and when are you going to do it?"

"I have my guitar lesson in an hour, so I'll do it after that."

"So by the end of the day, you're going to have all your laundry done and put away in the closet, with nothing left in the dryer?"

"Yes."

"And if tomorrow morning there are any clothes left in the laundry room, you agree we're not going to do anything else until they're clean and put away?"

"OK, yes." (Feel free to imagine the eye rolls.)

That is the Three Types of Agreement in action. Now, let's break down exactly what that means.

WHAT ARE THE THREE TYPES OF AGREEMENT?

*Agreements come in three varieties:
counterfeit, confirmation, and commitment.*

A counterfeit agreement from your counterpart is a fake yes just to placate you. A confirmation agreement reinforces the first yes and confirms that it was real. A commitment agreement further reinforces the previous yeses and establishes a real intention to follow through. Until you get all three, you don't have a solid agreement that you can trust your counterpart to follow through on.

It's easiest to understand this through an example. Let's say you're a potential client, and you and I have had a productive conversation about how we might work together. At the end, you say you'll take my proposal, think about it over the weekend, and share it with your team on Monday.

I say, "It sounds like you need time to ruminate on this."

"Yes."

"It also feels like the buck doesn't stop with you—there are people on the other side of the table who have to weigh in on this."

"Yes."

"So what you've told me so far is that you like my proposal, you want to think about it for a couple of days, and then you're going to present it to your team. And sometime Tuesday morning, I'll receive either a text or an email indicating what the next steps are."

"Yes."

That's my third yes. Now I'm much more confident that you're going to follow through because you've said yes three times in the same conversation about the same issue: our next steps. Plus, it sets me up to reach out to you on Tuesday afternoon if I don't hear from you, without feeling like I'm pestering you.

Notice that I used two Labels and a Summary to get those three agreements. You don't have to do exactly that, but it's a very effective strategy. If I'm getting Accommodator vibes from you, I'll shore up our agreement even more with a Calibrated Question (knowing that Accommodators are prone to overpromising): "If I don't hear from you by 1:00 p.m. on Tuesday, what should my next move be?" That's the binding glue. I would bet money that you'll reach out by 1:00 p.m. on Tuesday, even if it's just to say you need more time.

One crucial note: All these agreements have to occur in the *same* conversation about the *same* thing. That's what makes this different from the concept of yes momentum, the yeses that are all over the place and about different things—not building on each other the way these three agreements are.

Going for three agreements is so effective because most of us want to be consistent in our thoughts, words, and actions. When we're not, it causes internal conflict that makes us uncomfortable. By getting the person to agree repeatedly, out loud, to take specific actions, you make it harder for them not to do it.

Our advice? View every initial agreement you get as counterfeit. Test it as if it's bullshit, because it very well might be. Analysts are the least likely to give a counterfeit agreement, but it might sound like they're agreeing to something when they're really just agreeing to think about it. Assertives are known for making agreements without thinking about how to implement them. Accommodators are notorious for saying yes just because they don't want to disappoint you with a no.

In short, you can't trust any agreement that hasn't been thoroughly tested.

REAL-WORLD EXAMPLES

The Masonry Crew

A while back, there was a masonry crew doing some construction at my house. My wife and I were about to go away for two weeks, and they wanted to get paid before we left because they planned to finish while we were gone. I was nervous that if I paid them before the work was complete and inspected for defects, the job wouldn't get done right and I would have a hard time getting them to fix any problems we might find on our return.

My wife speaks Spanish, so she went to talk to them. The conversation went something like this:

"I'm going to pay you now. When I come back in two weeks, is the work going to be done?"

"Yes."

"And if I find that there's something that needs to get fixed, will you come back and fix it?"

"Yes."

"Are you a man of your word? Would your father say you're a man of your word?" (This was a bold move, but she made it with confidence because she knew these guys and understood their worldview. This kind of honor was important to them, and they would be very reluctant to do anything to contradict this claim, especially after they said it out loud to her.)

"Yes."

Two weeks later, we returned to find the work done. And in fact, something did need to be adjusted, and they came back to fix it without resistance or delay.

Calling Out a Counterfeit Yes

When I'm working with an EOS client, one of the most important elements of the session is deciding on the client team's "rocks." Rocks are tasks that the team is committed to accomplishing in the next 90 days, and each rock has one owner. That person might not be the only one working on the task, but they're responsible for seeing that it gets done.

From many years of experience, I know that in the process of determining the rocks, I'm very likely to hear some counterfeit yeses. Nobody wants to be the naysayer who says a certain task shouldn't be a priority when other people think it should. Nobody wants to be the one to admit they're not the right person to take responsibility for a given task. There's a huge amount of reluctance to upset the consensus or let the team down, so people often say yes to things they really don't want to say yes to.

That reluctance is obvious if you're paying attention to tone and body language. You know what an enthusiastic yes looks and sounds like. It doesn't include things like hesitation, uncertainty, hostility, shrugging, sighing, or avoidance of eye contact. I can't possibly list all the signs here, but you will know them when you see them—as long as you don't let happy ears blind you.

When I suspect a counterfeit yes, I don't let it slide. I call it out: "That sounds like a counterfeit yes." I'm essentially calling them a liar, which should be offensive, but people don't take it that way. In fact, they're usually relieved that I've sniffed out the truth, and they're grateful for the opportunity to explain their reservations. Everybody else in the room is relieved, too; they could sense the hesitation but didn't know how to address it.

When I use this phrase, it's usually in situations where I've already established strong rapport with the other person. If you haven't done that yet, you can opt for a gentler approach that achieves the same thing: Labeling their reluctance. This might sound like:

- "You don't sound very sure about that."
- "You seem hesitant about this decision."
- "It looks like you have some reservations."

Situations drive tactics; choose the words that feel like the best fit for your situation. Just don't let a counterfeit yes fly by unacknowledged. Call it out—everyone will be glad you did.

IN SHORT ...

- Agreements come in three varieties: counterfeit, confirmation, and commitment.
- A *counterfeit* agreement is a fake yes just to keep the conversation moving.
- A *confirmation* agreement reinforces the first yes and confirms that it was real.
- A *commitment* agreement further reinforces the previous yeses and establishes a real intention to follow through.
- Until you get all three, you don't have a solid agreement that you can trust your counterpart to execute.

LOW-STAKES PRACTICE

To start getting comfortable with the Three Types of Agreement, do these exercises.

1. **When you hear a yes, Label it.** Practice with small agreements, like your partner agreeing to pick up the dry cleaning. Don't take one yes for an answer. Respond by Labeling any hesitation you might (or might not) be sensing: "It sounds like you might have trouble fitting this errand into your day."
2. **Before ending a conversation, Summarize the agreement.** Again, practice this with small agreements first. To use the same dry cleaning example, you might say, "So what you've told me is that you plan to pick up the dry cleaning after work and you'll make sure your boss knows you can't stay late today so you can make it before the dry cleaner closes."

3. **Whenever you suspect a weak agreement, use Calibrated Questions.** Do this with anyone who has a history of not following through or who has agreed to do something you know they don't really want to do. Ask "what" and "how" questions to get them to articulate exactly how they will fulfill the agreement. To continue with the dry cleaning example, this might be something like, "What will you do if your last meeting of the day starts to run long?"

To learn more about the Three Types of Agreement, scan the QR code and join the Black Swan Community.

CHAPTER 18

NO-ORIENTED QUESTIONS

One day in the afternoon, I went with some clients for drinks at the Ace Hotel in New York City. We were able to secure a nice couch and table for the five of us, and I ended up having their special, limited-time cocktail, K-Pop Punch: vodka, brandy, Yakult, dairy, simple syrup, lemon, and passion fruit.

One of my clients had been peppering me with questions about Tactical Empathy for at least half an hour when the waiter came over to inform us that it was now happy hour and, unfortunately, the happy hour menu was limited to beer and wine.

Challenge accepted—I always say that every obstacle in life offers another opportunity to practice Tactical Empathy.

So, I looked at the waiter and asked, "How hard would it be to get another K-Pop Punch?"

He said, "Not hard at all," and proceeded to get me another drink. Upon his return, he told me it was on the house. With nothing but one simple question, not only did I get the forbidden drink, but I got it for *free*. The client's jaw was on the floor.

What was so special about that request?

It was a No-Oriented Question.

WHAT IS A NO-ORIENTED QUESTION?

> *A No-Oriented Question is a question designed to get a "no" (or otherwise negative) response, with the goal of protecting your counterpart's autonomy.*

When you ask a yes/no question, you always have two options about how to formulate it. The default is usually to ask it in a way that makes "yes" your preferred answer. However, you can always turn it around so that what you actually want to hear—what would serve your purposes—is "no." For example:

- "Is this a good time to talk?" →
  "Is this a bad time to talk?"
- "Are you ready for the next step?" →
  "Would it be a bad idea to move on to the next step?"
- "Is this a good idea?" →
  "Is this a ridiculous idea?"
- "Are you willing … ?" →
  "Are you against … ?"
- "Would you still like to … ?" →
  "Have you given up on … ?"

Why bother doing this? Because while we love to hear "yes," we hate to say it. We're battered by requests for "yes" all day, every day. Everybody from our loved ones to our colleagues to the ads on our screens wants us to say it. Every time we do, we feel like we're giving away a little piece of ourselves—our time, our attention, our energy, our resources.

And we should feel that way, because "yes" has, in fact, been weaponized against us. Just look at all the sales training out there about yes momentum and "tie-downs." Salespeople are taught to ask us questions we couldn't possibly say no to, under the theory that if we say "yes" enough times to small things, we're more likely to say "yes" to their big ask.

If you've ever been sold to before—and we all have—you've experienced this firsthand. Every "yes" they squeeze out of you feels more and more reluctant, and your resentment toward the asker builds up. Even if you do end up saying "yes" to the ask, you feel like you were manipulated into it, which makes it far more likely you'll backtrack later or find some way to punish them for dragging you in.

After a lifetime of this, we've been conditioned that "yes" is a trap. That makes yes-oriented questions threatening, even if only on a subconscious level. And as you know well by now, Tactical Empathy is meant to remove you as a threat to your counterpart in the conversation.

Saying "no," on the other hand, feels safe. It feels like we're protecting ourselves and keeping the demands of the world at bay. If we're already feeling defensive, "no" is the first thing on the tip of the tongue when someone asks a question.

That's why it's often a good idea to rephrase your yes/no questions as No-Oriented Questions. You allow your counterpart to say "no"—which is what they instinctively want to say—and still get the response that serves you.

WHY IT WORKS

You might be thinking this is silly. People aren't stupid—just because you switch the words around doesn't mean they won't realize you're asking for something.

You're right. Their logical brains will know that saying "no" to a No-Oriented Question puts them in the same position as saying "yes" to the yes-oriented version of that same question. But we're not concerned with what they're thinking; we care about what they're feeling. Emotions happen at a deeper level that's driven by instinct and conditioning, not logic. And at that level, it still *feels* better to say "no" than to say "yes," even if both lead to the same place.

To see what we mean, imagine that someone calls you out of the blue and asks, "You got a few minutes?" They've immediately sent the signal that talking with you is what *they* want, and when someone wants something from you, you instinctively get defensive. They called you because it's a good time for *them* to talk, and they're asking you to agree to their agenda. They clearly want a "yes," which makes it harder to say "no" because you know it will disappoint them.

Now you're thinking: *Do I have a few minutes? Do I want to spend them talking to you? Do I want to talk about what you want to talk about? How long is a few minutes anyway? How do I end this conversation?* All those things come to your mind in a nanosecond, and it makes you defensive.

Instead, imagine they call you and say, "I know I probably caught you in the middle of something. Is now a bad time to talk?" Now you feel you have options. You can say, "Yes, it's a bad time. I'll call you back." Or you can say, "No, I'm good for a couple of minutes. What's this about?" Both responses feel equally easy. You're in control of the conversation. They're deferring to your agenda.

A No-Oriented Question is not a magic bullet. It's not guaranteed to get you the answer you want. What it will do is help remove you as a threat and keep your counterpart from going into a defensive mode. Remember the analogy of chopping down a tree: Each use of a Tactical Empathy skill is a swing of the ax, and it's the combined power of many swings that achieves the goal. A No-Oriented Question is just one more swing of the ax.

REAL-WORLD EXAMPLES

How Hard Would It Be ... ?

I have a pilot's license, and a few months ago, I was flying a small plane from New York City to Traverse City, Michigan. To get out of New York City safely, I had to follow a very specific flight plan from air traffic control. However, once I was out of the metro area and flying over Pennsylvania, I could request permission to abandon the given path and just take the straightest path to my destination.

Most people would say to air traffic control, "Can I get direct to Traverse City?" There's nothing horribly wrong with that, and it might get a "yes." However, I wanted to maximize my chances. I knew that air traffic agents were in a stressful position, fielding requests all day long while trying to keep everyone safe. Their default position when it comes to making exceptions to rules and standard procedures is "no," and for good reason.

So, I turned my request into a No-Oriented Question: "How hard would it be to get direct to Traverse City?" This doesn't precisely follow the No-Oriented Question formula in that the answer I'm looking for isn't exactly "no"—it's something like "not hard at all." Still, it has the same effect in that it makes the other person feel like they genuinely have a choice. Derek's preferred version of this question would be "How bad of a position would I put you in if I asked for direct to Traverse City?" Same idea, slightly different wording.

It worked like a charm. "No problem," air traffic control told me. "Permission granted for direct to Traverse City."

Have You Given Up On ... ?

When someone is ghosting you, there's one No-Oriented Question that's almost guaranteed to make them reappear: "Have you given up on [fill in the blank]?" We teach our students that if they haven't heard from their counterpart in a while, they should send a subject-line-only email with this question. More often than not, people who have been MIA for weeks or even months respond within minutes.

We often test this at live events. Last year, I gave a talk to eighty of the top executives at JPMorganChase. At the beginning of the talk, I said, "This is going to sound crazy ... if there's anyone who has been ghosting you in a negotiation, I want you to send them an email right now, subject line only, that says, 'Have you given up on working together?' Do that right now, and if you get a response while I'm here on stage, I want you to raise your hand and interrupt me."

In the next sixty minutes, I got interrupted four times. Even more people came up to me throughout the rest of the day to show me the responses they had gotten. Some were positive about moving forward; others made it clear that the deal was dead. Either way, it was a win for the asker, who no longer had to waste time waiting and wondering.

IN SHORT ...

- A No-Oriented Question is a question designed to get a "no" response, with the goal of protecting your counterpart's autonomy.
- People hate to say "yes"—it leaves them feeling vulnerable and defensive, and they will often say "yes" without meaning it, just to placate you.
- People love to say "no"—it makes them feel safe and in control.
- Whenever possible, phrase your yes/no questions so that "no" is the response that serves your purposes.

LOW-STAKES PRACTICE

To start getting comfortable with No-Oriented Questions, do these exercises.

1. **"Would you be opposed to … ?"** When making an ask, instead of saying, "Can I schedule a meeting with you?" try, "Would you be opposed to meeting next week?"
2. **"Have you given up on … ?"** When following up on unanswered emails or messages, instead of saying something like, "Just checking in on the status of this project," try, "Have you given up on finishing this project?"
3. **"Would you be against … ?"** When asking for agreement with something, instead of saying, "Do you agree with this approach?" try, "Would you be against trying this method?"

To learn more about No-Oriented Questions, scan the QR code and join the Black Swan Community.

CONCLUSION

At the start of this book, I was an FBI reject.

A few months later, I was at an exclusive club in New York City, chatting with the assistant director of the FBI.

I was hosting a private party for Chris and a select group of my EOS clients—a chance for them to meet the master himself. That morning, Chris called me and asked if Mike could come.

"Who's Mike?" I asked.

"You know, Mike, the assistant director of the FBI."

So that evening, I'm sitting at the table with Chris and Mike, and I tell them, "You know, the funny thing is, I'm actually supposed to be in class at the FBI Citizens Academy tonight. I need to submit an excuse for my absence."

"Oh," Mike said, "you need evidence?"

So there I was, snapping a picture with Chris and Mike. Not such a reject anymore, and it was all thanks to Tactical Empathy.

In the very first chapter, we told you this book would be your companion on the journey to master Tactical Empathy. Well, now that you've reached the end of the book, we have some bad news...

That journey isn't over.

In fact, it will never be over. It isn't over for me, or for Derek, or even for Chris. We are all, every one of us, still practicing, learning, and refining our skills every day. We'll be doing that for the rest of our lives. That's the spirit of the proven process we talked about at the very beginning of this book, the cyclical path with four steps:

1. **Learn:** Build the foundation by engaging with resources—like this book—that give you information about the principles and skills.

2. **Adopt:** Let go of the traditional combative approach to negotiation and adopt the Tactical Empathy frame of mind for every sensitive conversation.

3. **Practice:** Practice the skills in low-stakes environments, log your efforts, and reflect on them to discover where you excel and where you need more work.

4. **Apply:** Use your skills in real situations where the pressure is on and the stakes are real.

The Japanese have a term that applies beautifully here: *shuhari*. It's a concept from martial arts that describes three phases of a lifelong learning process.

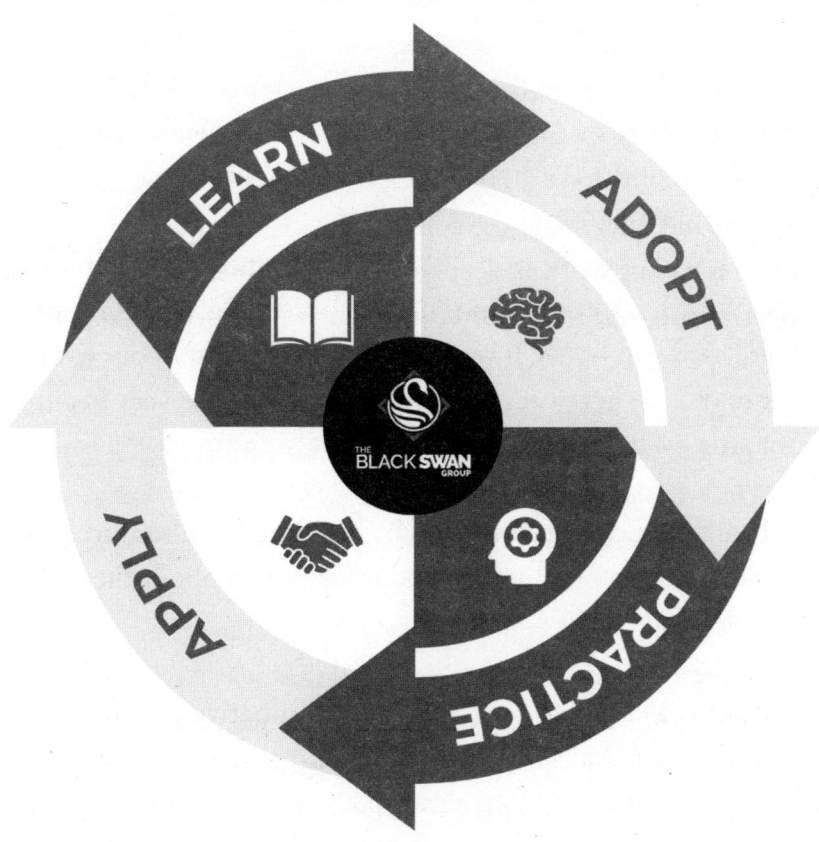

In the first phase, *shu*, you do exactly what the teacher tells you to do, exactly how they say. You don't ask questions about how or why. You just do it, over and over. Through repetition, you start to understand the meaning and reasoning behind what you're doing.

That's when you enter *ha*. In this phase, you explore the how and why more deeply. You begin to see not just how to do it but how to see *inside* it—how the parts fit together and work as a whole. You can start to test boundaries and intentionally break some of the rules.

When you've truly understood and mastered the skills from every angle, you enter *ri*. This is the phase where you can use your knowledge creatively. It's no longer about following strict processes but about honoring fundamental principles, no matter how off script you go.

Nothing about this lifelong learning process is automatic or easy. Like it or not, the Black Swan skills often go directly against what we've been programmed and conditioned to do our whole lives. That means we're working to erase very strong, very deep neural pathways and replace them with new ones. If we don't do the work to make those new pathways just as strong, the old ones will take over again.

Sometimes, that work is deeply uncomfortable. In fact, I think I've never been more uncomfortable in my whole life than when I went through the gauntlet to become a Black Swan coach. As a candidate, I had to "teach" each of the skills to the current coaches, and their job was to make my job as hard as possible. They questioned every little detail—*What about this? What if that? What would that sound like? What does that mean?* They wanted to make me sweat, and they succeeded.

What's more, I didn't nail it the first time. They sent me back to the drawing board on some of the skills—and that was part of the test, too. Was I humble enough to accept my deficiencies and work to correct them? Or was I going to get defensive and push back on their criticism? I knew that if I wanted to truly be a master, I had to be willing to keep learning, always, even when I had already worked so hard and learned so much.

From where you stand now, it's impossible to imagine how far you can go with these skills. Take Derek. He started learning them as a police negotiator more than thirty years ago. He used them masterfully to resolve hostage crises and save lives. But he looks back at those negotiations today and thinks, *If I could go back with the skills I have now, I wouldn't have spent seven hours talking that guy off the bridge—I would have gotten it done in three.*

One thing is for sure: No one is born with these skills. Some may have more of an aptitude for them than others, but *everyone* has to put in the hours of practice to gain proficiency ... and proficiency is just the beginning.

We said it in chapter 1, and it bears repeating here: Tactical Empathy is like a foreign language. The more you practice it and immerse yourself in it, the faster you'll learn. First, you'll become conversational—comfortable with the basics. Then you'll become proficient—capable of using all the elements. Then comes fluency, where it starts to feel natural and effortless. But even that's not the end, because there's really no limit to the mastery of a language. If you have the desire, you can elevate it from simple communication to true artistry.

Why bother with all this effort?

Because it will *change your life*.

The skills in this book have made a lot of money for the people who use them, and that's cool. But what really makes it rewarding for us as coaches is the impact these skills have on people's personal lives. Just think of it: What would it mean to have a happier relationship with your partner? To feel closer to your kids? To feel valued and understood at work? To build friendships you can really depend on? To move through the world feeling like people are opening doors for you instead of slamming them in your face?

That's the real power of Tactical Empathy ... and that's what this book can give you, as long as you don't put it on a shelf and forget about it. *Keep using it.*

Keep journaling every day.

Keep sharing your experiences with your Tactical Empathy peer group.

If you haven't already, read *Never Split the Difference* and watch Chris Voss's MasterClass.

Join us for an online workshop or a live training session.

When it comes to learning Tactical Empathy, there's no lack of education, support, or community. All you have to do is reach out, and it's yours. This is what immersion looks like. Commit to immersing yourself in these skills, and in a few years, you'll look back and wonder how you ever got by without them.

And when in doubt, remember the Tactical Empathy Pledge:

I will ...
stay curious,
remove myself as a threat,
proactively address expressed and unexpressed dynamics/emotions,
listen with purpose,
and practice Tactical Empathy as my superpower.

And I will ...

test all agreements,
Proof of Life every potential opportunity,
transform conversations into lasting relationships,
and not explain without permission.

And I will ...

hunt for black swans,
make "No" work for me,
and embrace the power of emotional buy-in ("That's Right.")

APPENDIX

AI AS A TACTICAL EMPATHY TOOL

You might be one of the many, many people who have started using artificial intelligence (AI) to help write emails, presentations, speeches, and more.

If so, you probably think we've been completely ignoring a crucial development in the world of communication.

You might even think we're *against* the use of AI in sensitive conversations.

In fact, AI—if trained properly—can be an incredibly helpful thought partner in mastering Tactical Empathy. Sensitive conversations are human-to-human interactions, and we would never advise outsourcing your side of the conversation to AI. However, an AI tool that has been explicitly trained in Tactical Empathy can help you prepare and practice for those sensitive conversations. AI can suggest which skills might be useful in a specific situation; it can brainstorm tailored Accusations Audits and Calibrated Questions; it can even listen to you vent and help you get into a state of curiosity.

In The Black Swan Group, we've developed several AI tools that help people learn and apply the skills in this book, and we're continually advancing and refining our use of this powerful technology. For example, Chris collaborated with MasterClass to create a voice-powered AI version of himself that you can talk to in real time. It answers your questions and gives you feedback, and it sounds just like the real Chris. We've also developed a custom GPT that generates a negotiation "cheat sheet" for you based on your description of the situation. It gives you a Summary, Accusations Audits, Calibrated Questions, and Labels you can use when you get in the room with your counterpart.

Find out more about our AI tools for Tactical Empathy—including our latest developments—at www.blackswanltd.com/ai. Again, there's no substitute for real, human empathy. However, these tools truly can help you expand your thinking and hone your skills in preparation for face-to-face conversations.

TACTICAL EMPATHY LOGBOOK

The negotiation skills outlined in this book don't stick unless you practice them. They are also perishable. Like a pilot logs flight hours to stay sharp, great negotiators need consistent reps to develop and maintain their edge.

We suggest setting aside fifteen minutes a day to use the logbook in this section to track your practice.

Each entry should include:

- Who you negotiated with
- The context or situation
- The specific Black Swan skill you used
- What the outcome was

For reference, there is a list of the chapters in the book on the next page if you need a refresher on the skills.

This type of practice turns small conversations into high-impact training and keeps your instincts sharp so you can perform when the stakes are real.

Start small. Reflect often. Build the habit—and the skills will follow.

CHAPTER & SKILL REFERENCE

PART I: THE BLACK SWAN METHOD

Chapter 2: Tactical Empathy
Chapter 3: The 5 Levels of Listening
Chapter 4: The Laws of Negotiation Gravity
Chapter 5: Black Swans

PART II: THE CORE FOUR

Chapter 6: Labels
Chapter 7: Mirrors
Chapter 8: Dynamic Silence
Chapter 9: Summary

PART III: THE BEST OF THE REST

Chapter 10: Accusations Audit
Chapter 11: Tone
Chapter 12: Calibrated Questions
Chapter 13: Encouragers
Chapter 14: "I" Messages and the Phases of No

PART IV: THE NEXT LEVEL

Chapter 15: Negotiator Personality Types
Chapter 16: Proof of Life
Chapter 17: Three Types of Agreement
Chapter 18: No-Oriented Questions

Tactical Empathy Logbook

Date

Counterpart(s)
Situation

Skills Used
Outcome

Date

Counterpart(s)
Situation

Skills Used
Outcome

Date

Counterpart(s)
Situation

Skills Used
Outcome

Date

Counterpart(s)
Situation

Skills Used
Outcome

Tactical Empathy Logbook

Date

Counterpart(s)
Situation

Skills Used
Outcome

Date

Counterpart(s)
Situation

Skills Used
Outcome

Date

Counterpart(s)
Situation

Skills Used
Outcome

Date

Counterpart(s)
Situation

Skills Used
Outcome

Tactical Empathy Logbook

Date

Counterpart(s)
Situation

Skills Used
Outcome

Date

Counterpart(s)
Situation

Skills Used
Outcome

Date

Counterpart(s)
Situation

Skills Used
Outcome

Date

Counterpart(s)
Situation

Skills Used
Outcome

Date

Counterpart(s)
Situation

Skills Used
Outcome

Date

Counterpart(s)
Situation

Skills Used
Outcome

Date

Counterpart(s)
Situation

Skills Used
Outcome

Date

Counterpart(s)
Situation

Skills Used
Outcome

Date

Counterpart(s)
Situation

Skills Used
Outcome

Date

Counterpart(s)
Situation

Skills Used
Outcome

Date

Counterpart(s)
Situation

Skills Used
Outcome

Date

Counterpart(s)
Situation

Skills Used
Outcome

Date

Counterpart(s)
Situation

Skills Used
Outcome

Date

Counterpart(s)
Situation

Skills Used
Outcome

Date

Counterpart(s)
Situation

Skills Used
Outcome

Date

Counterpart(s)
Situation

Skills Used
Outcome

Tactical Empathy Logbook

Date

Counterpart(s)
Situation

Skills Used
Outcome

Date

Counterpart(s)
Situation

Skills Used
Outcome

Date

Counterpart(s)
Situation

Skills Used
Outcome

Date

Counterpart(s)
Situation

Skills Used
Outcome

ACKNOWLEDGMENTS

This book represents the culmination of years of conversations, conflicts, corrections, and breakthroughs. It exists because of the incredible people who shared those moments with me—sometimes as allies, sometimes as adversaries, but always as teachers.

First, I want to thank my coauthor, Jonathan B. Smith. Your relentless curiosity and commitment to mastering Tactical Empathy took this book from concept to reality. A battle-tested playbook to help others get better. Watching your enthusiasm as you apply these skills in real time reminds me that what we teach isn't theory. It's how all of us should move through the world.

To Chris Voss—my friend, mentor, and fellow traveler in the discipline of negotiation. You helped me understand that influence is about making people feel heard, not pushing harder. That principle changed my life and has continued to change the lives of everyone I've coached or taught.

To the entire team at The Black Swan Group—Sandy Hein, Troy Smith, and every other coach and staff member who pushes these ideas further every day. You embody the mindset that Tactical Empathy isn't just a technique—it's a way of treating people.

To the thousands of professionals, leaders, and skeptics I've had the honor of working with over the years—thank you for challenging me to teach better, listen deeper, and never assume.

To my law enforcement family—especially the hostage negotiators of the Alexandria Police Department and the Alexandria Sheriff's Office—together we learned what pressure really feels like and what functioning proficiently as team despite it truly looks like. The lessons I learned managing crises with you remain the bedrock of everything I teach

And finally, to the readers willing to rethink how they speak, listen, and lead—you're the reason this book exists. May the pages you consumed help you fight less, win more, and build trust where others default to conflict.

Stay curious. Stay humble. And remember—it's not about you.

Derek Gaunt

This book is the result of years of practice, partnership, and pushing boundaries. It exists because of the remarkable people who've walked this path with me—mentors, teammates, clients, and friends—each one sharpening the blade.

First and foremost, to my wife Doris—my number one supporter, fan, and grounding force. None of this happens without you.

To Chris Voss—for inviting me into the Black Swan family and seeing the potential in our partnership before it was obvious. Your vision and belief made this possible.

To Derek Gaunt—PhD-level practitioner and steady hand. Your commitment to excellence ensured this book stayed true to the standard. It's been an honor to build it with you.

Acknowledgments

To Brandon Voss—your insight, generosity, and collaboration were instrumental in shaping the foundation of this book.

To the Black Swan team—Ken Williams, as our Integrator and General Manager, you keep the gears meshing and ensure every initiative runs flawlessly. Troy Smith and Marcella Oakley, as my Black Swan training partners, you took me from wide-eyed novice to confident practitioner, teaching me the art and discipline of Tactical Empathy at every turn. Thank you for being the backbone of everything we accomplish together.

To Brittany Alfson—for being the calm in the storm and keeping me on track every step of the way.

To Madison Fitzpatrick and the Amplify team—You were more than collaborators—you were true creative partners. Your talent for capturing our voice, clarifying complex ideas, and sharpening every sentence made this project possible.

To Chris White, Ken DeWitt, Joseph Kim, Mark O'Donnell, Marcello Dispensa, Matt Foss, Ben Berman, Andrew Brenner, Jeremy Olen, Dr. Sam Weinstein, Sam Garfunkle, and the Honey Badgers—your friendship, perspective, and thought partnership mean the world.

To the Stay Curious Cohort—thank you for holding space for deep work and shared growth. You challenge me to think sharper and lead better.

To Mary Pat Knight, Dr. Dino Signore, and Mark Huge—thank you for coaching me through the storms, plateaus, and breakthroughs.

And to all my clients—you've given me the real-world lab to test and refine these ideas. Your trust and time made me better.

Here's to fighting less, winning more, and staying endlessly curious.

Jonathan B. Smith

ABOUT THE AUTHORS

Jonathan B. Smith is a leading business strategist who has used the Entrepreneurial Operating System with more than 150 high-growth entrepreneurial companies in 1,500-plus sessions to help them improve strategy, execution, and results. He is also a negotiations trainer with the Black Swan Group, created by former FBI hostage negotiator Chris Voss (author of *Never Split the Difference*), and has served as a delegate with the U.S. Department of State's Global Entrepreneurship Program to Jakarta and Athens.

Derek Gaunt is one of America's top experts on hostage negotiation and a trainer and personal coach of corporate, government, and law enforcement personnel with the Black Swan Group. A twenty-nine-year law enforcement veteran who spent the majority of his career as a member and leader of hostage negotiation teams, he now teaches leaders around the world how to leverage hostage negotiation practices and principles for immediate results. He is a frequent keynote speaker at conferences across the country and the author of *Ego, Authority, Failure: Using Emotional Intelligence Like a Hostage Negotiator to Succeed as a Leader*.